KW-420-200

TABLE OF CONTENTS

Foreword by the Rt. Rev. Crispian Hollis, Bishop of Portsmouth ..... *i*

Preface ....*iii*

Introduction ....*iv*

Chapter 1   The Early Years – St. Joseph's Parish, Havant.................. 1
Chapter 2   The First Church Building. 6
Chapter 3   Birth of the Parish and the building of
             St. Michael and All Angels..................................... 10
Chapter 4   Growth to Maturity.. 16
Chapter 5   The Middle Years.. 21
Chapter 6   Fire and Destruction.. 28
Chapter 7   The Rebuilding of the Church.................................. 41
Chapter 8   The Parish Sisters and
             'The Sisters of Merriemede'...................................... 58
Chapter 9   Music in the Parish 60
Chapter 10 Symbols and Sacred Images in The Church 68

Appendices
   Appendix 1   Priests serving Leigh Park 80
   Appendix 2   Papal and Diocesan Awards 81
   Appendix 3   Works of Art in the Church................................. 83
   Appendix 4   The Mustard Seed 85
   Appendix 5   An Appreciation of John Burridge 87
   Appendix 6   Parishioners who have chaired the
                 Parish Council.. 88
   Appendix 7   Letters of Support and Donations
                 following the loss of the Church in 2001............. 89
   Appendix 8   The Relic of St. Anthony of Padua 90

Acknowledgements... 91

ILLUSTRATIONS

The first Church of St. Michael and All Angels 8

Interior of the first St. Michael and All Angels 8

The old Presbytery 9

The new roof is built onto the old Church 9

Front Page of the Portsmouth News 4th July 2001 26

The aftermath of the fire – the roof reduced to ashes 27

The aftermath of the fire – the sanctuary 27

The Church Hall reverts to the Church of St. Michael 32

The foundations for the new church 32

Parish consultations – Brian Maddock offers enlightenment 33

Neil Barr listens to Eileen Trodd 33

Paul Hazell takes note watched by Fr. Joe and Judy Stringer 33

The steel frame is erected..34

The cupola is constructed 34

Father Joe fixes the cross to the cupola 35

The new Church of St. Michael and All Angels 36

The new Church of St. Michael and All Angels - Western elevation 36

New Church interior..37

New Church interior – view towards the Narthex 37

The Sanctuary window..38

The Baptistry area...38

The Lady Chapel window 39

New Presbytery 39

Father Joe at the new Altar..40

Jim Berry and the new Church Organ 40

The Parish Sisters –

     Srs. Maria and Anne-Marie 56

     Sr. Michelle 56

     Sr. Suzanne 56

     Sr. Susan 56

     Sr. Christine...57

     Sr. Geraldine 57

     Sr. Marie-Therese 57

     Sr. Betty...57

W/D

Rosalind Maskell and Arthur Beardsley

St Michael's Publications

©Rosalind Maskell and Arthur Beardsley 2005
Birth and Rebirth of a Parish

ISBN 0-9550251-0-9

Published by St. Michael's Publications
83 Bramdean Drive
Leigh Park
Havant
PO9 4RR

A CIP catalogue record of this book
can be obtained from the British Library.

Design & production co-ordinated by:
The Better Book Company Ltd
Havant
Hampshire
PO9 2XH

Printed in England.

Cover photograph: Architect's sketch of the proposed church.

Symbols and Sacred Images in the Church
The Crucifix above the High Altar......................................65
The Celtic Cross in the High Altar......................................66
The Tabernacle, the IHS and the PX symbols......................67
The Ambo and the Alpha and Omega symbol.....................67
Ground Plan of the Church of St. Michael and All Angels..............70

Leigh Park Priests –
Father Murphy O'Connor...76
Father John Keenan...76
Father Pat Lyons...76
Father Hishon with Jo and Les Cannell.............................77
Father Dominic Golding...77
Father Peter Turbitt...78
Father Tom McGrath...78
Father John Dunne...78
Father Joseph Keller..79
Father Jozef Gruszkiewicz...79
Father John O'Shea with Laurie Stephens.........................79

Martha O'Connell and John Burridge display their awards.............82

Works of Art in the Church
The Blue Tiled Cross by J.L. Jezierski...............................84
The Icon of St. Michael...84
The Icon of Our Lady of the Holy Land............................84
The Book of Remembrance...84

Foreword by the Right Reverend Crispian Hollis, Bishop of Portsmouth

The celebration of the Feast of the Presentation of the Lord (February 2nd) in 2005 was one of the most fulfilling and enjoyable experiences of my life as Bishop of Portsmouth. On that day, not only were we able to celebrate and give thanks to God the Father for the gift of His Son, our Saviour Jesus Christ, but also we were able to make a very special presentation to the Lord in return. We were able to offer to Him a new home for the gathering of His disciples in Leigh Park.

July 4th 2001 had, in many ways, been a day of tragedy, and even despair, as many of us witnessed helplessly the destruction by thunderbolt and fire of the Church of St. Michael and All Angels. Perhaps not the most beautiful church building, it had nevertheless been the spiritual home and centre for the Catholic community in Leigh Park since it was opened in 1970. And now it was gone – and what would become of the community who had regularly gathered there?

From that moment when I stood and watched the blaze, I was determined that Leigh Park should have a new church. There were those who felt that perhaps this was the time to consider new buildings that could, perhaps, incorporate the parish with its neighbour at The Sacred Heart in Waterlooville. Without offering any disrespect to the people of the Sacred Heart parish, I knew that Leigh Park – almost more than anywhere else – needed and deserved its own church. This is why I was so full of joy when I came on February 2nd 2005 to dedicate the new church that had risen, like a phoenix, from the ashes and ruins of its predecessor.

That we have been able to realise this magnificent achievement is a huge tribute to all the dedicated men and women, priests and lay, whose deeds and commitment are chronicled in this history. What has been achieved is truly remarkable. At a time when the Church is said to be in decline, boldly to proclaim and celebrate the presence of

Christ's Church in Leigh Park is a wonderful tribute to God's grace working in the hearts and lives of so many people too numerous to mention.

This new church is a "light shining in the dark"; it is a place of warmth and welcome; it is a place of grace and life; it is a place where the disciples of Christ are to be found, gathering to celebrate the Eucharist and the saving presence of the Lord; it is a place from which those disciples will stream out to give witness and proclamation to the Gospel of Christ; it is, above all, a place of Communion and Mission, the very raison d'être of the Christian Church.

Bishop Crispian Hollis
Bishop of Portsmouth

PREFACE

With the perspective of history, it is possible to see that life is a never ending struggle between the forces of good and evil, and that out of bad events good things can come. At such times God speaks to us and inspires us to build anew.

The history of St. Michael and All Angels is a story of how, at the end of World War II, the people of Portsmouth, having endured great destruction of their city through bombing, set out to rebuild their shattered communities in the green fields of Leigh Park. It is a story of how that community has since grown and evolved.

Three years ago in 2001, the Church was struck by lightning and burned to the ground in the ensuing fire. It seemed for a while that all was lost. However, a new community spirit emerged with a determination to build a fine new church. As part of this new spirit a Parish History was planned. At my request the project was taken on by Rosalind Maskell; in recent months she was joined by Arthur Beardsley. I thank them and all who have contributed in any way to the book or to the rebuilding of the Church.

I hope that the book will inspire present and future generations of parishioners to appreciate and understand our Church. To this end I have added a final chapter on the signs and symbols in the Church.

Father Joe Gruszkiewicz, Leigh Park, 2005

INTRODUCTION

During the years following World War II many new Catholic churches were built to accommodate the increasing Catholic population. The Second Vatican Council turned the attention of the Church authorities to the need to reconsider traditional designs in order to implement increased participation by the laity in the Liturgy. In general, decisions were taken by Diocesan authorities and lay people played little part in the design process. Even in an enlightened parish and diocese such as Leigh Park and Portsmouth it is apparent that decisions about the design and building of the first church were taken by the Diocesan authorities, the Parish Priest and the Architect. Lay people played an important part in the practicalities of the building and, most remarkably, in actively taking on some of the construction, notably of the Presbytery, themselves. The congregation was privileged to have a new church built to the requirements of a changing world. Most unusually, though, the fact that that church was destroyed by fire in 2001 has given them the opportunity to design and build a new church in tune with the very different requirements of today. This double opportunity in the lifetime of one congregation must be unique.

Cars, shops, television and other facets of life which nowadays claim the attention of people were almost completely absent from the lives of those who lived in Leigh Park in the earlier days of the parish. At that time the Church fulfilled many of the functions which now occupy the spare time of parishioners. Factors such as bus times were those that influenced decisions about Mass times, whereas now Mass is provided on Saturday evenings to allow of sporting and other activities related to the increasing secularisation of Sundays. However, it is important that such considerations are not a source of disillusionment in the parishes of today. The world has changed and Catholics must change with it. Rather than bemoaning the disappearance of parish life of earlier days, we must adapt if we are to retain as parishioners those young people who, year by year, their parents present for Baptism and First Communion. Their new tastes and freedom from parental discipline must be harnessed in a way that capitalises on their positive qualities; the health of a parish can be gauged by the way in which they achieve this.

Chapter One – 1950 to 1954

The Early Years – St. Joseph's Parish, Havant

Leigh Park, a large house situated in nearly 2000 acres of land to the north of Havant in Hampshire, was purchased by Sir George Staunton from the Bishop of Winchester in 1827. He spent his leisure time creating the magnificent gardens which remain today and are being restored to their former splendour. The original 18th century house was pulled down by his successor, William Stone MP, and replaced by another in the Victorian Gothic style. In 1875 the house and estate were sold to the FitzWygram family who first encouraged the use of the gardens for children's outings and other events, not only for the people of neighbouring Havant, but from further afield in Portsmouth.

In 1940 the Admiralty requisitioned Leigh Park House for use by the mine department (U.C.W.E.), their research section being sited at nearby West Leigh House. It was in 1943 that Portsmouth City Council first considered Leigh Park as a possible site for the development of a Garden City. It envisaged 'a group of villages clustered around a central civic and shopping area'. The proposal was approved by the government in the same year. A year later the council paid £122,465 for 1672 acres – £75 per acre – the majority being purchased from Parkleigh Investments, the then owners.

The size of the proposed development alarmed the members of Havant and Waterlooville Urban District Council, who decided to oppose the plans at every opportunity. Nonetheless, the purchase of the land was finalised in 1945. Leigh Park House was itself used by the Admiralty until 1956, at which time the Portsmouth City Council decided that it had no public use for the building. The Parks Committee announced their intention to retain the house and grounds as an open space. Having fallen into a state of disrepair Leigh Park House was demolished in 1959.

The large number of people made homeless by the bombing of Portsmouth during the Second World War, and the steadily increasing number of returning servicemen, posed a serious housing problem for the area. One immediate solution was to use the naval camps in Leigh Park, and the first residents were moved into these Nissen huts as temporary accommodation. The huts were occupied not only by Hampshire people but also by Polish, Lithuanian, Latvian and Estonian refugees forced to flee their country during the war. These refugees were to form an important part of the growing Catholic population of the area.

On the 15th September 1947 the Lord Mayor of Portsmouth started the machine which cut the first sod to open the first trench for the house building at Leigh Park – 'this land of hope and promise'. It was to become the largest residential housing development in Europe. The original plan was that the estate should house 23,000 persons and, by 1953, 3,491 housing units had been completed. By the early 1970s the population had grown to 39,000. In 1948-9 people began to move into the first houses in Bramdean Drive and around the Riders Lane area as others started to occupy houses in the Stockheath area which was being developed by Havant Council. There were no schools, shops, doctors or chemists for them and most of the men made long journeys in to work in Portsmouth each day. Mothers pushed prams through the mud as they took their children to schools and surgeries in Havant, Waterlooville and Cowplain. It would be some time before conditions improved as the estate developed.

The population of Leigh Park grew rapidly from its beginning in the late 40s and churches in the neighbouring towns wondered how they could serve the people. At first the few Catholics walked to Mass at St. Joseph's in West Street, Havant, where an old white haired priest, Canon Bailey, always gave Holy Communion before Mass. He died, and in 1950 Canon Scantlebury was appointed parish priest. One of his first actions was to found a branch of the Legion of Mary, giving them the task of taking a census of all Catholics then living in Leigh Park. Writing at that time in St. Joseph's Parish Jottings he said *"The estates at Leigh Park are an ever-gnawing problem. I feel sure that a post-mortem would reveal those two words deeply engraved on my heart. Waking or sleeping, my mind seems always preoccupied with LP. The Legion of Mary canvassing constantly discovers more and more Catholics, and large numbers of them are small children. Mothers with families of toddlers find a difficulty in getting to Mass, particularly as there is no bus service on Sunday mornings. Our School is not big enough to take all the children, so there is their religious instruction to be considered. What is to be done? Attempts are being made to organise a Catechism Class for children there on Sunday afternoons, and I am hoping it may be possible to start Sunday Mass there too. That would mean obtaining the services of another priest, which in turn means more expenses, both for the hire of the hall and for the priest's attendance. The Sunday collections have a multitude of things to cover!"*

John Waller, one of the founder members of the Legion of Mary who is now living in Rowlands Castle, remembers the founding of the first Mass centre. He and a fellow member, Billy English, visited Mr. Gardener who was secretary of a Boy's Club held in part of the Stockheath Camp, a collection of Nissen huts situated in the original Riders Lane. This lane ran eastwards alongside the site of what was later to be developed as the Tambrands factory. They arranged to rent a Nissen hut for Sunday afternoon Catechism classes and these started in April 1951. The rent of the premises was ten shillings (50 pence) per week. Sixteen children were taught by Sister Saint Columba who travelled out from the Convent of the Helpers of the Holy Souls in Mile End, Portsmouth. The classes were taken over by the members of the Legion of Mary in October 1951.

On the 30th September 1951 Canon Scantlebury spoke from the pulpit about the future for a church in Leigh Park. *"The problem of Leigh Park weighs heavily on your Parish Priest's conscience. An effort is going to be made to have Sunday Mass there, possibly beginning on a Sunday in December. All the requisites for an Altar have to be obtained. One of the biggest items is a new Missal. This costs about £12. Would anyone like to present a Missal or any of the other things for the Altar of the Holy Sacrifice?"*

In November he gave thanks to *"all those who have so devotedly worked to prepare the chapel at Leigh Park."* He mentioned *"the generosity of Mr. John Parnell, the practical help of Mr. John Waller and the generosity of the ladies who have given donations towards the new Missal."* On the 9th December 1951 Mass was said in the Nissen hut for the first time and from then onwards it was said weekly on Sundays.

By 1952 the growth of Leigh Park had made the parish of Havant too big for one priest. Canon Scantlebury went to the Seminary at

Wonersh, chose a student he liked the look of and then told Bishop King that he wanted a curate. In July the student, now a priest, arrived. It was Father Targett and very soon the Catholics of Leigh Park felt that they had a priest of their own. Father Targett, who had been a magician in the variety halls and later a prisoner of war, worked there with such untiring dedication that many older Catholics today remember the time with great nostalgia. In 2002 Father Targett, now living in retirement in Oxfordshire, wrote to the author *"I came, newly ordained, to Havant parish in the summer of 1952 and left in the autumn of 1958. The first task given me by the Parish Priest was to make a parish register for Leigh Park by house to house visiting. I completed this in just a few months. It was, of course, at a time when a priest could go visiting at any time of day and nearly always find somebody at home. My visitations were blessed with quite a few converts and the blessing in the Catholic Church of many marriages originally celebrated in churches of other denominations. I also met many wonderful people like the Wallers who have kept in touch all these years."* (One of these visits also eventually resulted in the vocation of Father Michael Peters to the Priesthood, the only vocation known to the authors to have come from Leigh Park.) *"In 1924 another priest was doing the same thing visiting from house the house in SE London. At our house he found a family where the husband was a lapsed Catholic and none of the three sons had been baptized. He arranged for them to be baptized and transferred to the Catholic schools. Years later one of the boys decided that if he ever got out of the prisoner of war camp he would become a priest and is now hoping you can read his horrible handwriting."* He continues *"One of my most vivid memories of the ministry in Leigh Park before the church was built was a Christmas Midnight Mass celebrated in the old Nissen hut with an old iron stove in the middle with the chimney pipe going up and out through the roof and people huddled round it for warmth."* Writing of those days some years later, Laurie Stephens, one of the early parishioners and later Headmaster of St. Thomas More's School and organist and choirmaster of the new Parish Church, recalled the days in the Nissen hut. *"It was somewhere between Swanmore Road and Winterslow Drive, at that time just trees and narrow lanes that were ankle deep in mud in winter. We sat on hard benches, smoked out if we lit the stove, frozen if we didn't, while the condensation dripped on us from the roof. We watched the priest at the dull brown triptych altar brightened by a white altar cloth embroidered in red and we enjoyed the presence of God."*

Soon Canon Scantlebury persuaded Archbishop King to buy a site in Dunsbury Way for a church for the future Leigh Park parish. In his parish notices of August 1953 he reported on progress with the new Church Hall, a project for which the Havant parishioners had to raise money at the same time as that needed for an addition to the parish school. The Canon commented on 'red tape worse than the Hampton Court Maze' but permits were obtained. He estimated that £4,200 would be needed for the building. The St. Joseph's Development Society had been formed, a football pool was started and the parishioners were informed that 'everything was legal and above board'. In June 1954 the first demand for payment of £500 was received and in July the Canon reported that the Hall was going up. The sum of £900 had been raised by the football pool during the previous year. The extension to the School provided ninety new places and Catechism classes at Leigh Park were then discontinued. At that time the average Mass attendance at Leigh Park was 125 people.

Chapter Two – 1954 to 1966

The First Church Building

The Hall was built by Marchetti and dedicated to Blessed Margaret Pole (the martyr who was executed by Henry VIII in 1541 and who had lived at Warblington, to whom Archbishop King had a special devotion). The first Mass was celebrated there on Christmas Eve 1954. Even with the erection of this building conditions were far from ideal. Canon Scantlebury remembered how, week after week, his car used to get bogged down in the mud in the land surrounding the Church. He always had to get together a party of men from the congregation to help him on his way back to Havant after Mass. Later a rota of Havant parishioners was arranged to drive the Canon to and from Mass at Leigh Park.

Another apparent difficulty arose over the building by an American company of a factory opposite the Church. Canon Scantlebury was told that planning permission for the factory had been refused because of its position in relation to the Church. Mystified, the Canon said that he could not think how that would matter. Then the dreadful truth was revealed: the factory was to be for the manufacture of tampons, the use of which was then considered a mortal sin. Horrified, Canon Scantlebury felt he could not withdraw the permission he had already given for the factory to be built. But it took a special theological document sent from America by the Director of Tampax to convince him that no mortal sin was involved. In the event the relationship thus formed with the management of the factory was to prove useful when the new church was being erected.

In August 1955 the average Mass attendance was recorded as 187; by 1959 it had risen to 240. In 1962 an extra Sunday evening Mass was started. Laurie Stephens remembered *"We did all the things Catholics like to do for their Church. The women polished the floor; the men put up a notice board; we even had a male voice choir for Holy Week. Rumours began that Father Targett was to be our parish priest but nothing came of it. In 1957 a third priest arrived, young and smiling – Father Bennett. In 1958 Father Targett (sadly) left us and Father Dobbin took his place. Then in 1962 Canon Scantlebury, who had grown tired of counting all the pennies in*

Birth and Rebirth of a Parish

the Leigh Park collections, went to Brockenhurst and Father Murphy arrived. He surprised us by entertaining us all (about 1,000) to dinner at Kemballs in Southsea as a way of initiating 'Planned Giving' in the parish". At that time there were an estimated 2,000 Catholics living in Leigh Park and the projected cost of the new church there was £40,000. Laurie Stephens continued *"Father Dobbin was replaced by Father Richer, very tall and thin, and he in turn, by Father Doran and then Father Keenan. During these years our longing for a 'proper' church grew. We wanted to be a parish. And in 1966 it happened. Father Patrick Murphy O'Connor came from Winchester and after a few weeks was made Parish Priest with Father Keenan as curate".*

By 1965 the estate at Leigh Park had grown to about 27,000, more than trebling the original parish of St. Joseph's. Although St. Joseph's was served by two priests there was also the Church at Emsworth to support and the time had come to consider alternative arrangements.

The first Church of St Michael and All Angels

Interior of the first Church of St Michael and All Angels

The Old Presbytery

The new roof is built onto the old Church

Chapter Three – 1966 to 1970

Birth of the Parish and the Building of St. Michael and all Angels

On Ascension Day in 1966 the Parish of Havant which had nurtured the fledgling church finally ceded responsibility and Leigh Park became a parish in its own right. Father Patrick Murphy O'Connor and Father Keenan set up house at 458 Dunsbury Way (later to become Great Copse Drive) where they were cared for by Mrs. Muriel Randall. When Father Keenan was moved to Bracknell in 1969, Father Pat was joined by Father John Dunne who had just been ordained. In 1970 Father John O'Shea arrived, also newly ordained. Both he and Father Pat left the parish in 1971.

Over this period the priests achieved much, notably the building up of a special sense of community amongst the parishioners and the realisation of their dreams of a new church. The sense of community was achieved principally by visiting parishioners in their homes and in gaining their co-operation in a multiplicity of activities, not least of which were social occasions for people of all ages. As Father Dunne remembers *'Father Pat so loved a parish party as a means of bonding parish life'*. Amongst those who helped in these activities were Mr. and Mrs. Wincza, Mr. and Mrs. King, Mr. R. Gill, Mr. Carolan, Mr. Leahy, Mr. Breslin, Mr. Mullins and others, including the Parish Sisters whose names will appear in later chapters. Family groups, the old and the young, Brownies and Guides; all were catered for and the clergy played a full part in ecumenical relationships with those of other faiths. Father Dunne writes *"Father Pat had a tremendous understanding of the Universal Church and was also very committed to ecumenism. Implementing the guidelines of the Second Vatican Council was a priority in his ministry. Apart from parish life he had a number of Diocesan responsibilities; he particularly supported the idea of parishes working together. A man ahead of his time."*

Money, of course, was seldom far from the minds of the clergy who, at that time, bore the whole of the responsibility for the financial affairs of the Parish. This burden was later to be shared with the laity and Father Pat enlisted early on the help of many of the parishioners. An Outdoor

Collection was started in April 1967 and a weekly draw in 1968. Ten laymen took on the responsibility for the Outdoor Collections; they went from house to house collecting half-crowns (twelve and a half pence in today's money). This sometimes required great generosity from people who were living on very low incomes. The names of some of these laymen have already been mentioned; others included Mr. J Sinclair, Mr. T Leahy, Mr. J Kirby, Mr. P O'Kennedy, Mr. J Cowell, Mr. W McClean and Mr. J McConigle. Father Pat stressed that this was not a formal committee and he hoped that *"later on a more representative committee will be formed including, of course, some of our hard working women parishioners."* As this history will show, these years marked a turning point in the attitude of the Church to the role of women who were, in time, to assume significantly greater responsibilities and functions in the life of the parish.

Father Pat's commitment to Leigh Park, its people and its Church is best expressed in his own words: *"A Priest has his special commission from God – so have you as a layman or laywoman. Our Lord has asked us to preach the Gospel to every creature. He has asked us to look after the poor, the hungry, the sick and old. We cannot just be preoccupied with our New Church, important though it is – our New Church is to be the source of strength and grace, as our Church Hall is, the place where we gather on Sundays and weekdays to worship God as a family. At Mass we share in the sacrifice of Christ together – we must learn to continue outside the Church to work together for the spread of God's Kingdom in our own hearts and the hearts of others."*

The New Church

In 1967 the contract for the building of the new church, to be called the Church of the Ascension, was awarded to the architects, Wearing, Hastings and Rossi of Norwich, the partner in charge being Anthony Rossi. The building contract was awarded to John Hunt Ltd. From then on a long and detailed correspondence between Father Pat Murphy O'Connor and Anthony Rossi ensued. Much had to change between that time and the eventual opening of the church. An initial estimate of the cost of the Church and Presbytery, including external works, organ and church furnishings was £92,410, a long way from the £40,000 projected by Canon Murphy in his Planned Giving Prospectus! There were many reasons for this escalation of cost, including the devaluation of the pound by Harold Wilson's government in 1967. After many economies, including a decision that much of the work on the inside of the Presbytery should be carried out by volunteer parishioners, the eventual cost, including the organ and other fittings, was pruned to about £75,000. The cost was originally supported by a loan from the Diocese which had, of course, to be repaid eventually by the Parish. In the event, over the years this debt was added to by the expense of repairs to the Church, (in particular those due to a leaky roof, dating from even before the Church was opened, leading to the eventual replacement of the flat roof by a pitched one) and by necessary alterations to the Church Hall.

Money was raised by the Outdoor Collections and Weekly Draw, by the traditional Christmas and Easter Fairs, by letting the Church Hall for various purposes and from individual donations. Prominent among the latter were regular contributions (£2,000 in 1967 and several others later) from Thomas F. Casey, Chairman of the American parent company of the Tampax factory which was sited opposite the rising church building. A parishioner recalls that a flag was hoisted above the factory when Mr. Casey was visiting from America; seeing this Father Pat would telephone for a chat to report progress and a further donation was often forthcoming! Another substantial source of funds was a bequest to the Diocese of £21,000 for the building of a church dedicated to St. Michael and All Angels. At the time the need of Leigh Park was greatest in the Diocese and it was decided to change the dedication of the Church from the Church of the Ascension to St. Michael and All Angels. The original intention was to open the church on Ascension Day 1969 but in the event this was delayed until May 1970.

At a time of great liturgical changes in response to the Second Vatican Council and in view of the character of the buildings on the Leigh Park estate into which the Church must blend, the traditional cruciform design hitherto associated with churches was not considered. An octagonal design capable of seating 320 people in the main worship area around the altar was adopted. Originally the architect planned a pyramid-style roof but, in the end, a flat roof was fitted. This change brought with it many problems throughout the lifetime of the building.

Although he was aware of the need for economy and to pare expense to the minimum Father Pat was intent that some items of real quality should be included in the Church. He commissioned a two-manual pipe organ from Walker and Sons Ltd. of Ruislip, which was built at a cost of just under £7,000 in March 1970, providing a suitable vehicle for the considerable musical skills of Laurie Stephens, the Parish Organist and Choirmaster, who had composed a version of the Mass in English which was sung for many years after he had left the parish. A bell was commissioned from the Whitechapel Bell Foundry and a striking blue ceramic Crucifix from J.L. Jezierski. The latter formed a focal point on the wall at the west end of the Church, behind the seating for the celebrants. Modern statues of Our Lady and St. Joseph were installed on arrangements of painted metal pipes. The latter conformed to an ephemeral fashion of the day and were not to the taste of many parishioners; they were later removed and replaced by more conventional plinths.

Building began in February 1969 and the Foundation Stone was laid by Bishop Worlock in July of that year. It was made of grey marble and contained two sealed lead capsules, the contents of which are still a mystery. This stone was subsequently saved from the fire in 2001 to be incorporated into the new church that was eventually to rise from the ashes. The main building was completed by November 1969.

On the 15th May 1970 the Church, packed to capacity, was solemnly blessed and opened by Bishop Worlock. The parish clergy were joined by several other priests who had served Leigh Park from Havant in its early days – Fathers Targett, Bennett, Richer and Keenan. In the evening a celebratory party was held at the Tampax factory. At the time the Church was opened the population of Leigh Park was 39,000 of whom 2,500 were known Catholics. Six hundred attended Mass regularly.

In view of the fact that the church building itself was considered to be of such importance in the life of the Parish and knowing, with hindsight, that it would be destroyed in 31 years time when there would be very different requirements for its successor, it is interesting to quote from an account written by the Architect at the time of its opening in 1970.

"The estate has no heart and tends to lack a sense of time and place. The exterior of the Church building is deliberately designed as a simple dominating mass of good quality dark brickwork to contribute a feeling of permanence and character. The two turrets with the bell and the Cross help to express its purpose and to project the Church visually into the community; a function fulfilled audibly by the bell, ringing for the Angelus and for service times, placed at the most dominating corner of the site. Internally the plan consists of a low roofed octagon with three smaller semi-octagonal areas attached to it on three sides. These three areas are the Presbytery, the Blessed Sacrament Chapel and the Meeting Room, the last being linked to the existing church hall. Between the Presbytery and the Blessed Sacrament Chapel is the Sacristy with access to both these and the main space. The main octagon, seventy feet across, is for the celebration of the Parish Liturgy on Sundays and Holy days but, since all items of furniture are moveable, it may also serve for Parish general meetings, religious concerts, plays or other suitable functions. Thus there is within one building a complete and flexible parish centre. The architectural treatment is of the utmost simplicity, with whitewashed concrete block walls, a steel 'factory' roof and a plain hardwearing floor finish. The small amount of richness in the furnishings is reserved for those items directly connected with the celebration of the liturgy – rich hardwood for the Altar, lectern, sedilia, font and organ console, gold coloured nylon carpeting on the platforms and a rich blue ceramic crucifix, ten feet high, which dominates the interior. While most furnishings are moveable, flexible and of timber, the Blessed Sacrament Altar is of stone to give a sense of permanence to the 'rock of salvation' and this permanence is also expressed in the Foundation Stone in the floor of the main octagon, which is of the same grey marble."

The Presbytery

The shell of the house was provided as part of the main building contract and, in order to save money, a team of volunteer craftsmen under the leadership of Mr. Des Cleife offered to do some of the interior work themselves. This team included Mr. Cleife, himself a plasterer and carpenter, Mr. N King, a traffic warden but also a competent electrician, Mr. P Carolan, a plasterer, Mr. D. Hartley, a Dockyard plumber and coppersmith, Mr. G Burrows, an electrician and Mr. R Gill, a factory supervisor. Others gave a helping hand as and when required. Work continued on Saturdays and at other odd times in order to get as much as possible done in the shortest possible time. In accordance with the Architect's plans the three-storey octagonal building was to have four bedrooms intended to house three priests with a separate flat for the housekeeper. The Presbytery was not yet ready for occupation when Father Pat and Father John O'Shea left the parish in 1971 and it was left to Father Llewhellin (who replaced Father Pat as Parish Priest) and Father Dunne to be the first occupants in 1972.

Another party of part-time workers started transforming the adjoining building, the original Church, to become the Church Hall.

As a result of all this voluntary work an estimated saving to the Church funds of £6,000 to £7,000 was made.

Chapter Four – 1970 to 1976

Growth to Maturity

With the arrival of Father John O'Shea and the realisation of the new Church, parish activities flourished. The choir, thirty strong, included Father Pat. John Burridge organised the Altar servers. Des Cliefe oversaw the building and repairs.(From the very beginning there were leaks through the flat roof, some of which were attributed by the architects to punctures resulting from stones being thrown onto it!). Dick Gill supervised the Planned Giving which was directed towards paying off the debt to the Diocese of £40,000 as well as supplying the needs of the priests and parish. Joyce King ran the Union of Catholic Mothers and Rose Gill, Georgina Shipman, June Smith and Sybil Wincza organised the Guides and Brownies. Norman King was in charge of entertainments and outings.

Sister Helen MacDonald of the Convent of the Helpers of the Holy Souls, Mile End, gave religious instruction to about 200 children who were not in Catholic schools. In time she also set up the Social Bureau in the Hall. This was open from Monday to Friday from 10 am to 12 noon and from 2 pm until 4 pm providing readily available help for many people. The professional services of Social Security, Health and Housing Departments could be called upon as necessary. Sister Helen had previously worked in San Francisco, Chicago, Camden Town and Portsea. Writing in 1973 she said that the problems were similar there to those she encountered in Leigh Park. Boys, girls, men and women of all ages and all denominations came to the Social Bureau seeking help with their problems or just wanting to pour out their tales into the ears of a sympathetic listener.

Family groups met in one another's houses to discuss issues such as teenage violence, sex and marriage, the priesthood, new forms of worship and many others. Indeed, the parish of St. Michael's could be said to have been well ahead of its time.

In 1971, Mass at St. Michael's was televised by Southern Television. The celebrants were Father Pat Murphy O'Connor and Father John Dunne. The Commentary was given by Father Cormac Murphy O'Connor, who, many years later, was to become Archbishop of

Westminster and a Cardinal. On the Feast of Corpus Christi in 1972 Mass from St. Michael's was transmitted live on BBC Radio 4. Father Llewhellin was the celebrant, Father Dunne preached and the action of the Mass was described by Father Patrick McEnroe, who was also the producer.

In 1971 Father Tony Llewhellin had arrived to replace Father Pat, who moved to Southampton. Father O'Shea also moved on. The feelings of the people were described so well by Laurie Stephens in the Mustard Seed (Appendix 4). Father Dunne remained and the two priests moved into the new Presbytery in 1972. They were joined in 1973 by Father Tom McGrath. At that time the Parish Registers show that there was an estimated Catholic population of 2,460, of whom about 550 attended Mass regularly. These numbers fell gradually over the next thirty years to an estimated Catholic population of 2,000 with about 200 regular Mass-goers.

The Parish Council, constituted by Father Pat at a time when such bodies were rare in the Catholic Church and both the clergy and laity were feeling their way, thrived. Initially chaired by Laurie Stephens it continued under the chairmanship of other dedicated parishioners (See Appendix 6).

West Leigh

When the Diocese bought the site in Dunsbury Way it also acquired a site on the east side of the Petersfield road. It was hoped that a church could be built there to serve the growing population of West Leigh. In the meantime, the priests would say Mass on Sundays in Sharp's Copse School. Few people had cars in those days and buses were at inconvenient times, making the journey to St. Michael's or St Joseph's in Havant, difficult. Monica Jacobs and her family moved from Yorkshire to live in West Leigh in 1973. She writes *"We arrived in Holy Week feeling a bit bewildered and isolated. Knowing that contact with the Church community and taking part in the familiar liturgy would make us feel more at home, the family of Mum, Dad and five children between the ages of three and ten years, set out for St. Joseph's in Havant on Good Friday. From the windows of the bus we caught sight of St. Michael's, gathered up the children and walked there. Immediately I felt at home and at peace. After the* service Father Dunne spoke to us, welcomed us most warmly and told us about the Mass at Sharp's Copse school on Sundays. Once the Easter ceremonies were over we started attending Sharp's Copse. I became a reader and the boys all became altar servers once they had made their first communion and had undergone thorough training by John Burridge. Our daughter, Margaret, could not understand why she was not allowed to be a server. Times have changed since then! Her consolation prize was to be allowed to blow out the candles after Mass and to help with stripping the altar and folding the altar linen. The Carolan and Leahy families were the backbone of the Church in West Leigh. The caretaker of the school, Mr. Bailey, would help them to set up the school hall for Mass. He would clear away afterwards and would never make us feel pressured to rush off quickly. One of the members, Robert Lee, played the piano, so whenever he was there we would have hymns. He eventually left the Parish to become a Brother in a religious order. Father Tom McGrath, who had replaced Father Dunne in 1972, celebrated the Mass at West Leigh. Whenever he visited his native Ireland he would return inspired by the lively musical liturgy there. He would try to similarly motivate and lead us. Sadly, as he would admit, singing was not his forte so music did not feature prominently in our services! On one memorable Sunday, due to a series of misunderstandings, Mr. Bailey did not arrive to open up the school. It was a beautiful sunny day and the priest decided to celebrate Mass in the open air under a tree.

Some children from Catholic families attended Sharp's Copse school. Sister Suzanne from Merrimede set up a small group of children under seven. I would meet them weekly in the school for 'God Talk' as a step towards preparation for their First Communion. For their parents it was a step that could, if they chose, ease their journey towards membership of the faith community of St. Michael's. As a community in West Leigh we did not feel separated from the main parish. We attended St. Michael's for major liturgical celebrations. We were, of course, part of all parish social and fund-raising events."

The proposed church at West Leigh was never built. By 1974 the maintenance of the site was costing the parish about £600 a year. The Parish Council asked the Bishop to give permission for the land to be sold back to the Borough Council. With a shortage of priests it became necessary to reduce the number of Masses said in the Parish and the West Leigh Masses came to an end. There was some protest and resentment since most of the community were old people and young families. The bus service to the parish church was poor and did not coincide with Mass times. A minibus was borrowed and driven by volunteer parishioners on a rota basis. It picked up senior citizens and the disabled. The 'Tribe of Jacobs', as Monica describes them, just had to get themselves more organised. The twenty five minute walk to the Church in all weathers was a challenge to be met. *"We could not afford to be late as the four boys were now serving and did not want to bring down upon themselves the wrath of John Burridge. Standards had been set and must be adhered to."*

Wings

The Parish magazine, entitled Wings, first appeared in October 1972 and then monthly until July 1974. It was founded and edited by Konrad Machez, a teacher at Wakeford School in West Leigh and virtually ceased when he moved away from the district. Some parishioners have kept all their copies and they make fascinating reading. In addition to parish news and announcements each issue carried a letter from the Parish Priest (Father Llewhellin throughout that time) and a thought provoking editorial on a topic of concern to the parishioners, for example, giving practical information about Lenten ecumenical groups. There were accounts of parish activities written by those concerned with them, for example the Social Bureau and Religious Education; reports from the Parish Council; notices of times and places of clubs and meetings; a calendar of events on the back cover and more light-hearted features such as recipes and drawings for the children to colour. Reading through the copies of the magazines one is struck with a nostalgia for days when teachers had time and inclination to produce a monthly edition, when partnerships of priests and people could have such a fruitful effect on parish life and the astonishing number of enterprises and opportunities which were available to parishioners.

After Konrad's departure no layman or woman could be found to take on the onerous task of Editor and Father Llewhellin made attempts to bring out the magazine himself. A few odd issues have survived since Konrad's last one (Number 19) and the final issue came out in

1977 during the time of Fathers Lyons and McElhinney. Subsequently parish information appeared in weekly newsletters. In 1981 one such edition listed the names of thirty-six parishioners responsible for twelve activities: typists, duplicators, baby sitters, transporters, hostesses, display team, poster makers, handymen, photographers, flower arrangers, outing organisers and altar servers!

Chapter Five – 1976 – 1997

The Middle Years

1976 to 1983

In 1976 Father Pat Lyons came to the Parish in place of Father Llewhellin and was himself succeeded by Father Ronald Hishon in 1980. The latter had returned to the Diocese from the Diocesan mission in Bamenda and left St. Michael's to be Rector of the English College in Valladolid in 1983. Few records of this period remain. Father Lyons died in 2003.

In October 1981 Bishop Emery celebrated a special Mass to commission the teams of Catechists and Music Makers for the parish. The Director was Sister Michelle and the Chief Catechist was Sister Maria. The Catechists were: Coralie and Bob Carter, Lucy Cliefe, Cathy Graham, John Grist, Marie Henderson, Monica Jacobs, Glen Kerridge, Eileen Leib, Yvonne Philip and Judy Stringer. The Music Makers were: Polly Alexander, Angela Burns, Lucy Cliefe, Kay and John Grist, Margaret Hurry, Jacqueline Hurry, Margaret Jacobs, Margaret Murphy and Laurie Stephens.

1983 to 1997

By 1983 when Father Peter Turbitt arrived to replace Father Hishon there were no longer enough priests in the diocese to provide for an assistant priest in the parish. From then onwards, apart from two brief periods, the Parish Priest lived alone in the Presbytery built for three priests.

During the years of Father Turbitt's incumbency there were some important landmarks. The flat roof continued to leak in many places as it had done almost from the beginning. In 1985 the decision was made to replace it with a pitched roof and the work was carried out during 1987-88. The architect was John Wingfield of Kanavan & Wingfield and the builders were Speltham Contracts Limited. In 1988, before the work was completed, there were already further leaks! The work was financed by a loan from the Diocese and despite regular repayments this loan is still outstanding today.

In 1986 an important change to the Parish boundaries was made. Rowlands Castle was geographically closer to St. Michael's than to St. Joseph's in Havant whilst remaining officially in the Havant parish. In fact, many of the Catholics living in Rowlands Castle attended Mass in St. Michael's and some were contributing in many ways to parish life there. The position was regularised by the Diocese in 1986. The northern boundary, which had previously been drawn through Southleigh Forest north of the West Leigh development, was moved to include Durrants and the whole of Rowlands Castle.

Father Turbitt accompanied groups of parishioners on two Pilgrimages. In 1987 they travelled to Rome for the Beatification of several English and Welsh martyrs. The next year a large party went to the Holy Land. This included visits to Gethsemene, Cana on the Sea of Galilee, the Mount of Olives and the Cedron Valley, Mount Carmel, Emmaus and the Dead Sea and the Al Aksa Mosque. Father Turbitt celebrated Mass in the Church of the Last Supper.

It was during Father Turbitt's tenure that Coralie Carter started using the Presbytery for marriage counselling through the Catholic Marriage Advisory Council. She kept up this service until her death in 2001.

In 1989 Father Turbitt moved to become parish priest of Wantage and his place at Leigh Park was taken by Father Felix Muscat, who had just returned from the Diocesan Mission in Bamenda, Cameroon. His incumbency at St. Michael's was to be the longest of any of the previous Parish priests although his leaving was a cause of much distress in the Parish. His incumbency was studded with landmarks of improvement in parish life for he had a talent for getting the advice and co-operation of many different kinds of people. Felix writes:
"After completing six years missionary work in the Archdiocese of Bamenda in Cameroon, West Africa I was appointed to succeed Father Turbitt at St. Michael's. I was officially installed in November 1989 by the then Vicar General of the Portsmouth Diocese, Monsignor Cyril Murtagh. On arrival at Leigh Park I was a stranger in a very close-knit community. I was touched by the very warm welcome I received. I was advised by three of my predecessors that the community at St. Michael's would be a joy to work with. They were absolutely right. Not only was it a joy to be part of that community but also

a privilege and a blessing. I was also given a warm welcome by the other local Christian communities, in particular St. Francis and St. Clare Church of England and the Methodist Church in Botley Drive. One of the first persons to greet me at the Presbytery on my first full working day was the vicar of St. Francis who brought me a bottle of wine. From the beginning of the opening of the Leigh Park estate ecumenical relations with the other Christian communities have been good. On numerous occasions we presented a common front in dealing with local social issues, such as establishing a local Credit Union, providing the young people with recreational facilities and supporting any programme aimed at dealing with drugs, unemployment and crime. We had monthly meetings of the priests and leaders of the local Christian churches and on special occasions we participated actively at each other's religious services. The tradition of the annual Mass in May at Warblington Church in honour of Blessed Margaret Pole was continued and was sometimes celebrated by Bishop Crispian, Bishop of Portsmouth.

Now that Rowlands Castle had been incorporated into the Parish, in order to establish a bond between the Catholics there and the rest of the parishioners, I started to celebrate Mass in the Congregational Church on The Green. This monthly celebration made it possible for some parishioners to get to know each other and it brought back to church a handful who had become lax about attendance at Mass.

I resigned from the active priesthood in December 1997."

A moving tribute was written by a parishioner and published in the newsletter:

"When Felix Muscat came to St. Michael's, Monsignor Murtagh, who introduced him, laid great emphasis on his youth; but since that day eight years ago Felix has served us in the parish with a maturity far beyond his years. In our griefs he has wept with us; in our joys he has laughed with us; in the confessional he has been wise and compassionate; at the altar he has been profoundly prayerful; and his sermons have been an inspiration.

He leaves behind a parish which is quietly loving and caring; and although it's well organised, it has not one scrap of officiousness which can so easily become the ugly companion of efficiency. Some of the credit belongs to us, but most of it belongs to Felix and to the quiet and unassuming way in which he has steered us all – nearer to each other and, above all, nearer to God. The French have a saying "To go away is to die a little", and Felix will certainly have died a little in leaving us – as indeed we have died a little in losing him. We can give him no finer memorial than to continue in the mould which he has done so much to form; quietly loving God in Himself and in each other."

During the years of Father Felix's incumbency there were many highlights, including the Ordination of John Chadwick in 1995, the Blessing of the Book of Remembrance on All Souls day 1992 and the Silver Jubilee Mass in 1995 at which the main celebrant was Archbishop Derek Worlock of Liverpool, a past Bishop of Portsmouth. John Chadwick had, before his ordination, lived at the Presbytery as Deacon to Father Felix and so was considered the 'local boy made good'. He writes *"I arrived at St. Michael's during July 1991. The Diocese recommended the parish for me as a home-base during holidays from the Seminary. For the next three years St. Michael's became precisely that, my home. With the benefit of Felix's guidance and support I learnt first hand what being a community priest was all about. Through his commitment to the people here in Leigh Park I learnt the importance of community in the life of a parish. St. Michael's provided the space for me to grow in my understanding of what I should be doing in life. In a very real sense, the experience led me to a greater understanding of God and his will for my life.*

After three years at St. Michael's and five years of training at Allen Hall Seminary in London, I was ordained deacon in Westminster Cathedral by the late Cardinal Hume. Two coach-loads of parishioners attended the celebration at the end of February 1994. This exemplified for me the commitment shown by the people of the parish during my time there. One year later, we celebrated my ordination to the priesthood at St. Michael's, which I know left a very deep impression on so many people.

I am so grateful to this unique community for giving me so much. I will never let go of my roots in Leigh Park."

A very welcome visitor to the parish was Father Michael Gedge, who came out of retirement at an advanced age, to say Mass in the absence of Father Felix. He had known the parish since its earliest days, being a close friend of Father Pat Murphy O'Connor.

Following the hiatus of Father Felix's leaving, the parish was rudderless for a period and a number of 'fill-in' priests, including Bishop Crispian, led the Mass on Sundays until a replacement could be found. Eventually Father Dominic Golding took up the reins. Father Dominic writes: *"When the Bishop asked me to cross the A3 from Waterlooville to Leigh Park my immediate response was to ask 'Do I have to?' This lack of enthusiasm stemmed from knowing my time as the assistant at Waterlooville was already coming to an end. I had no wish to bring the date any further forward. However, recognising the pastoral need I agreed to go and am certainly glad I did. My stint at Leigh Park only lasted eight months but it was undoubtedly an enriching experience. I came to love the parishioners for their honesty in serving the pastoral needs of the parish and for their energetic participation in my homilies. The depth of faith in this community was readily apparent. I remember standing Sunday after Sunday with them around the altar and recognising my love for them growing ever deeper. They fed my faith in ways for which I remain grateful. On the Sunday I took my leave of them to begin studies in canon law in Canada, I concluded my homily with these words 'my fondest memory will be of seeing us all gathered here each Sunday as the Church. Gathered in a building which enhances our worship. Gathered as a people who seem proud to belong here. Gathered as a people who, as I have discovered these last eight months, take ages to give each other the sign of peace. Gathered as a people who some weeks don't seem to want to go home. Those things have proved to me how committed you are to the practice of your faith. I hope and pray you will continue to be known for these qualities. May Jesus Christ never be just your hobby. May you and I remain proud of our faith and go on being His disciples.'*

The day the new church is consecrated will be a proud day and one I look forward to sharing in."

THUNDERBOLT HITS CHURCH

Thick black smoke engulfs the sky above the church at Leigh Park after the lightning strike

PICTURE: NEWS READER PAUL BURROWS

THIS was the scene today just moments after a bolt of lightning blasted through a church roof, turning the building into a blazing inferno.

Seventy firefighters fought the blaze at St Michael and All Angels Roman Catholic Church, at Leigh Park, in the middle of a heavy thunderstorm.

On-lookers told how they saw a flash from the sky, then smoke started billowing from the church roof and the building burst into flames. Children from the neighbouring pre-school building were evacuated as mothers ran from their homes to collect their youngsters who they feared had been injured in the fire.

There was no-one in the church when the lightning bolt struck but paramedics were on stand-by.

FULL STORY ● Page 5

Front page of the Portsmouth News 4th July 2001

Birth and Rebirth of a Parish

The aftermath of the fire – the roof reduced to ashes

The aftermath of the fire – the sanctuary

Chapter Six – 1998 to 2001

Fire and Destruction

Father Dominic departed from the parish in September 1998 to continue his studies in canon law in Canada for a period of two years. Once again John Burridge was left to find 'fill-in' priests for a period until it was announced that Father Joseph Keller would be taking over the parish on a permanent basis. Father Keller had been seconded to the Diocese from the Liverpool Diocese in exchange for a priest who had temporarily been assigned to Liverpool in a specialist capacity, so there was a degree of impermanence about his appointment as he would eventually be returning to Liverpool. However that was for the future and major events would eventually determine how the parish would develop. Father Keller assumed responsibility for the parish in September 1998.

Father Keller had been a late entrant to the priesthood, being ordained in 1993 at the age of 52. However he brought a zeal to the parish with a particular concern for the young who responded well to his interest. He forged strong links with the schools of St. Thomas More and Oaklands and conducted regular sessions with the pupils in raising their religious faith. It was unfortunate that his arrival coincided with a further reduction in active participants in the Mass and it must have been a difficult period of assimilation. Parish finances had been on a knife edge for a number of years, particularly following the requirement to service the loan for the new roof in 1988, and the reduction in numbers contributing to the collection had a serious impact. Father Keller's response was that he could live on virtually nothing and without doubt his living expenses were the lowest on record and somehow the books were balanced.

Father Keller's health was not good and there were numerous occasions when he should not have conducted Mass but he persisted, sometimes to the alarm of the congregation who were concerned about his welfare.

The Catholic Church in the Czech Republic and its struggles to maintain its existence since the post war period were of particular concern to Father Keller. He used his annual leave to visit the Republic and although severely cash constrained himself he made every effort to help the ordinary families. He encouraged the visits of Czech priests and in particular the visit of Fr. Pavel Kopecek in August of 2000. He was keen to hold a Mass in Czech one Christmas but was dissuaded from holding this in public. He also had links with Poland, spending his annual leave there in 1999. Was this a harbinger of things to come?

Father Keller was a supporter of the Tridentine Mass and a number of Sundays were reserved for the celebration of Mass in Latin during the year.

It was during Father Keller's incumbency that, after a number of attempts over the years, a grant was obtained from the 'Millennium Festival Awards for All' for £4,794 to install a toilet for the disabled in the Hall. Together with almost £3,000 that had been collected for this purpose, this made it possible to complete the installation in 2000.

Father Keller wrote in an Easter address to the pupils of Oaklands school, *'I enjoy being a priest and always make sure that I am seen in my uniform, the so called "Dog Collar". Even when I board Czech Airlines for my holiday in Praha, I am seen for the person I am − a priest. People remark that this plane journey is sure to be safe, and the people next to me always want to talk to me about my job. I have been Hospital Chaplain to the Maternity and Children's Hospital, plus various general hospitals, and − wait for it − a Prison Chaplain at Durham. Hence when I am asked "Is being a priest a bore?" The answer is No!'*

Being a priest was certainly not a bore on the 4th July, 2001. In fact the excitement was too much. Father Keller had just finished morning Mass at about 10.30 a.m. and was tidying up inside the Church. The playgroup, comprising about fourteen toddlers and their carers, were in the Church Hall adjoining the Church. The sky darkened and without warning a lightning bolt struck the Cross at the apex of the church roof and within seconds the roof was ablaze. The roof, which had been an addition to the flat roofed original church buildings, was a mass of wooden timbers inside and the original flat roof had been removed when the new roof had been built leaving only a thin ceiling to the church. Flames and smoke quickly engulfed the Church and thick black smoke fell down and flooded into the building. Fr. Keller was inside the Church when the lightning struck. He said *'There was just one massive bang that afterwards made me think, "Why am I still alive?"Within ten seconds the flames spread across the roof and my immediate problem was to get to the nursery school in the neighbouring building and get the children out.'* No-one was hurt as the group organisers led the toddlers to the canteen of the Proctor and Gamble plant opposite until all the parents arrived.

Watched by hundreds of local residents it took up to sixty fire-fighters over two hours to control the blaze and when eventually it was possible to assess the damage it was clear that there was almost total destruction. The roof was completely gone and although the walls were still standing there were large cracks down the full height. The church organ worth over £100,000 was destroyed. Everything in the Presbytery, which was an integral part of the building, was lost including Fr. Keller's personal possessions. Most of the church contents were lost but some of the precious items survived the heat and water to be rescued for restoration and reinstalment in a new church. Among these was the mosaic of St. Michael which, although damaged, was repairable and will feature in the new church.

Visiting the site later in the day, Bishop Crispian Hollis sent a message of support to the parish saying *'I was devastated to hear of the fire and I've been to see the damage and it is very extensive with the whole roof gone and cracks in the external walls. Fortunately Mass had just finished and there was no one in the Church. I have spoken with Fr. Keller and a number of parishioners. The congregation at Leigh Park is very resilient and I know they will rise to the challenge this disaster has placed upon them.'*

Response from the community was immense with letters of sympathy and donations flooding in from far and wide. (See list at Appendix 7) Fr. Keller wrote an open letter to the press a week later which fully expressed the parish's feelings. He wrote:

'Last week the Roman Catholic Church of St. Michael & All Angels at Leigh Park, Havant, was destroyed by a lightning bolt and ensuing fire, rendering the church and attached house unusable. The event was covered in a very sensitive and sympathetic way for which we are most grateful.

Birth and Rebirth of a Parish

In the aftermath of the event we have been almost overwhelmed by the outpouring of expressions of concern, letters of support, phone calls, donations and offers of help.

We are most appreciative of the many who have helped us to come through this tragedy.

In particular, we would like to express our great thanks to the local churches of Leigh Park and Havant, especially the Anglican Church of St Francis at Riders Lane and the Leigh Park Baptist Church.

St. Francis has been kind enough to allow us to use their church for Masses on both Saturday evening and Sunday morning, and done their utmost to make us feel at home there.

The elders of the Baptist Church have been outstandingly generous with their support too.

We are eternally grateful.

Despite the destruction of the buildings by the fire, through divine protection and the sterling work of Hampshire Fire Service and the salvage teams, many precious things have amazingly survived the heat and water, much to the relief of all our parishioners.

We now look forward to building a fine new church over the next year or two.'

It is ironic that Fr. Keller was due to end his secondment to the Portsmouth Diocese in July and would therefore take no part in the rebuild.

As mentioned in Fr. Keller's letter, the Anglican Church of St. Francis offered their church for the celebration of Mass and the first Masses held there were events of great emotion for the parishioners. In the event it was to be December of that year before the parishioners could return to St. Michael's with the bringing into use the church hall as a temporary church, the church hall that had been the original church building until 1966!

The Church Hall reverts to the Church of St Michael
The foundations for the new church

Parish consultations – Brian Maddock offers enlightenment

Neil Barr listens to Eileen Trodd *Paul Hazell takes note watched by*
Fr. Joe and Judy Stringer

The steel frame is erected
The cupola is constructed

Father Joe fixes the cross to the cupola

The new church of St. Michael and All Angels

The new church of St. Michael and All Angels — western elevation

Birth and Rebirth of a Parish

New church interior

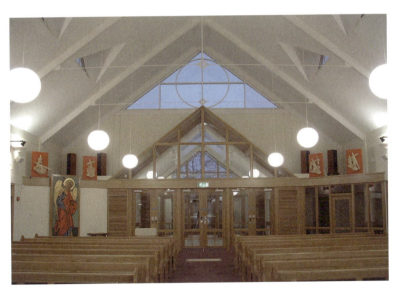

New church interior – view towards the Narthex

The Sanctuary window

The Baptistry area

Birth and Rebirth of a Parish

The Lady Chapel window

The New Presbytery

Father Joe at the new Altar

Jim Berry at the new Church Organ

Birth and Rebirth of a Parish

Chapter Seven – 2001 onwards
The Rebuilding of the Church

St. Francis Church, Riders Lane, under the incumbency of the Rev. Jonathan Jeffrey, was a kind host to the dispossessed congregation of St. Michael's. It couldn't have been easy to accommodate two services on a Sunday in the limited time available and the car park became very congested at times. This did not prevent the hosts from encouraging St. Michael's congregation to gather in the church hall after Mass for a cup of tea or coffee so helping to keep the parish together. As a consequence, both sets of parishioners got to know each other very well, a boost for ecumenical relations within the Leigh Park area.

It was into this environment that Father Jozef Gruszkiewicz arrived to lead the parish in late July. He had previously been parish priest in Gosport and had been in the Portsmouth Diocese for a number of years after serving as a missionary priest in Africa. A Polish national, he retained his allegiance to his Polish Bishop, but the parish were assured that his was a permanent appointment with the task of getting the new church underway. It is fortunate that the Rev. Jeffrey was happy to continue with the sharing arrangement at St. Francis as the possibility of bringing the church hall of St. Michael's into use was still some months away.

The Bishop of Portsmouth, Rt. Rev. Crispian Hollis, was determined that St. Michael's should be rebuilt and Father Joe was to be the key to this. When he spoke to the parishioners gathered for Mass in St. Francis, the Bishop made it clear that rebuilding should be treated as a great challenge for all involved, not just the rebuilding the bricks and mortar, but also rebuilding the flock, the spirit, morale and commitment too. The parish was fortunate in that the Diocesan insurance policy with Catholic National Mutual of Guernsey would be expected to cover the cost of the rebuild. However the effects of the disaster would be felt by the Diocesan parishes for years to come through increased premiums.

The first step was to find somewhere for Father Joe to live and a house was rented in Stockheath Lane, some three quarters of a mile away from the church site. Then followed the formidable task of clearing up the mess and arranging for the salvage and storage of the rescued items, supervising the securing of the site prior to demolition of the destroyed church and the conversion of the old church hall into a temporary church. Work was commenced on clearing the access to the hall and its refurbishment and restoration to the church that it once was. Father Joe's objective was that the parish would be able to celebrate Christmas 2001 in its own home and this was achieved with a couple of weeks to spare. The Christmas Masses were very cramped for space but this all contributed to a wonderful sense of relief. The parish had a home again.

In the meantime the Diocesan staff commissioned a study by the Quantity Surveyors, Northcroft, into the cost of rebuilding the old church and the cost of building a smaller church to a newer design on the old site. The findings of this study were presented to a meeting of the Diocesan representatives on the 23rd October 2001. The cost of rebuilding the church to the same design as the old church was estimated at £1.5 million which was the upper limit of what the insurers might support. After subtracting the cost of demolition and fees etc, the build cost for the church and presbytery was assessed at £1.15 million. It was decided to proceed on the basis of a new build of a church about three quarters the size of the previous building. This would have a significant financial effect, not least because a new build would be zero rated for tax whereas a rebuild of the old church would have incurred Value Added Tax at the rate of 17.5%, a cost of some £200,000. It was also decided that the Presbytery would be separate from the church building. The demolition contract was agreed, together with the proposal for the hall refurbishment.

Approval from the Insurers through the loss adjusters, Gordon Colbourne of Miller Fisher, was received on the 20th November to proceed with full demolition of the old buildings and to proceed on the basis of a new build for the church and presbytery. This cleared the way for the Diocese and the Parish to formulate their ideas as to what the new church was going to be like.

Father Joe's first task was to form a working committee of ten parishioners to provide the driving force behind the design and building of the new church. This committee was made up of the following:

Arthur Beardsley	John Burridge	Lucy Cleife
Paul Hazell	John McManus	Carol Maddock
Brian Maddock	Colin Newman	Dave Philip
Joan Wren.		

Carol Maddock was appointed to the Chair and Paul Hazell took on the responsibility of Deputy Chair and Secretary. The first informal meeting of this committee was held in December 2001, but it was not until the second meeting on the 13th December that the ground rules were laid down as to how the committee would cooperate with the Diocese. A provisional programme for the rebuild was proposed as follows:

Decision on choice of architects	February 2002
Architects to submit outline plans	May 2002
Complete design and obtain planning approval	July 2002
Tenders for the build	August 2002
Start build	September 2002
Completion	August 2003

An appeal was started to raise funds for the renovation of the hall. It was also agreed that the parishioners would be consulted on what kind of church and facilities they wanted. The questionnaire to determine these views was issued to parishioners at the Masses over the weekend 22nd/23rd December, and the results were assembled in time for the next meeting of the committee on the 24th January 2002.

To help the committee in its task of formulating ideas as to the design of the new church a series of visits to newly built churches in the diocese was arranged. On the 16th January seven members of the committee spent a very full day in visiting the churches of Our Lady Help of Christians in Farnborough, Our Lady Queen of Apostles in Bishops Waltham and The Immaculate Conception and St. Joseph in Christchurch. The committee was well received and was impressed by the enthusiasm shown by the representatives of each parish. Each church was very different, and it was an extremely useful exercise in determining what, and what not, to plan for in the new project. The committee met to consider the St. Michael's parishioners' preferences and to determine the outline specification of the church and presbytery. It was at this point that Dave Philip produced a sketch plan of a proposed layout and this plan was useful in polarising the committee's views of the design requirements This plan was, subsequently, to prove very close to the final design. Following further meetings an 'Outline Requirement for the Rebuilding of St. Michael's Church' was produced on the 8th February. This envisaged a church in a traditional style, an essentially rectangular exterior shape with an internal layout in cruciform shape and a sloping tiled roof. The building should be in brick to match the surrounding area and should have a bell tower. The church should be capable of seating up to three hundred people with the main nave accommodating two hundred in permanent seating. A large porch area was necessary as a welcoming area and for socialising after mass. Community rooms should be separate from the worship areas but connected with the church hall. More detailed requirements specified the liturgical aspects, the atmosphere and the ambience sought. The Presbytery should be a separate building on the same site.

In the meantime the Diocese had arranged for a meeting to review the contenders for the architects for the project. On the 20th February five firms made their submissions in the presence of:

The Vicar General, Rev. Mgr. Canon Jeremy Garrett. Chairman

Rev. Canon Alan Griffiths, Liturgical Advisor

Mr. David Rogers, Diocesan Building Advisor

Mr. Iain McGrory, Financial Secretary

Rev. Jozef Gruszkiewicz, St. Michael's Parish Priest

Mr. Sean Hayes, Diocesan Surveyor

Dr. Paul Hazell, St. Michael's BC Deputy Chair

Mr. John McManus, St. Michael's BC Structure

Mr. Arthur Beardsley, St. Michael's BC Finance

The contending architects were:

Sue and Paul Masser of Masser Architects

Birth and Rebirth of a Parish

John Wingfield and Tony Kanavan of Kanavan and Wingfield
Sandy Brown of the Solway Brown Partnership
Rex Butland and Oliver Freeman of the New Sarum Partnership
Ben Krause and Neil Barr of Daniel Lelliot Krause

Three of the presentations were considered very good and the architects felt they could deliver, although the target cost of £1.15 million, the figure considered acceptable to the Insurers, was very tight. It became clear, however, that an August 2003 completion date could not be achieved and that the summer of 2004 was more likely. At a subsequent meeting to consider the findings of the interviews it was agreed that three of the architects be invited to submit detailed proposals for a feasibility study by the end of May. The three practices were Daniel Lelliot Krause (DLK), New Sarum Partnership and Massers.

The building committee continued the work of refining the requirements for the new build and it was not until the 16th May that the final version was approved. This was sent to the three architects as the basis for their submission of proposals for a feasibility study for consideration at a Diocesan meeting fixed for the 24th June. The parish committee met beforehand to consider the architects' submissions with the outcome that the committee's nomination was DLK. The meeting with the diocesan representatives under the chairmanship of Iain McGrory confirmed the choice of DLK as the first preference and agreed to commit to a feasibility study at a cost of £900. The involvement of consulting engineers, the Andrew Newby Partnership, and Northcroft, the quantity surveyors, in the study was agreed.

The parish committee met to prepare a Statement of Requirements for the feasibility study which was finalised at a meeting with the Diocese on the 3rd July, and DLK were subsequently contracted to commence the study on the 16th July with the object of completion by the end of September.

The architects, Neil Barr and Richard Gale of DLK, first met the full parish building committee on the 8th August and presented three interim proposals for the committee to consider. The committee strongly favoured the first option but were warned by Malcolm Austin of Northcroft that the preliminary estimate placed this above the figure likely to be acceptable to the insurers. However, it was decided to move ahead on the basis of this option provided that costs could be reduced to an acceptable figure. This was confirmed at a meeting with the Diocesan Planning Committee on the 21st August. It was also confirmed that the new loss adjuster would be Mr. Steve Aldersley who was starting with a clean sheet. The previous loss adjuster, Miller Fisher, now in liquidation, had lost the file relating to St. Michael's claim!

Ongoing consultations with the architects and specialists resulted in further refinements of the proposed Church and Presbytery. The total ground floor area had been settled at 850 square metres at a cost slightly in excess of £1.4 million. The Diocesan Liturgical Advisor, Canon Griffiths, was generally in favour of the scheme but had detailed comments which needed to be addressed. A further meeting with DLK and Northcroft on the 18th September took account of the recommendations of Canon Griffiths. The final draft discussed with the parish committee a week later indicated that the cost had now risen to £1.724 million, a figure not acceptable to the loss adjuster. As a result DLK had produced a fall back option reducing the scale of the building to give a revised costing of £1.55 million. The committee were unhappy with this situation, being firmly of the opinion that the loss adjuster was undervaluing the alternative cost of a rebuild of the old church against which the budget was being compared. However DLK were committed to complete the study, and the feasibility study was finally issued on the 26th September 2002.

Dave Philip reluctantly resigned from the parish committee at this time as he was leaving the area. His contribution to the work of the committee was warmly applauded.

The parish committee met with the Diocesan Planning Group on the 10th October, and were pleased to hear that the parish's preferred option had been accepted by the loss adjuster at an all up cost of £1.68 million, giving an effective build cost of £1.3 million. The committee was charged with the task of identifying cost reduction proposals of up to £80,000 to incorporate in the final design, and to produce detailed estimates of the contents of the old church to progress the contents claim with the loss adjuster. The organ in the old church had been insured for £53,000 although its replacement value was more than double this. The loss adjuster was prepared to recommend settlement at £53,000 with the parish being able to use any surplus money available after the purchase of a modern electronic organ for its own use. (An important point if there was to be an overrun of costs.) The Chairman of the Diocesan Planning Committee confirmed he would be recommending approval to proceed to design stage to the Diocesan Finance Committee later that month. A letter of intent was issued to DLK in November, nine months later than originally envisaged.

The parish committee continued to work with DLK to refine the build specification and to prepare the way for submission for planning consent to Havant Borough Council. A presentation of the proposals to the parishioners was held in early December which proved very animated. DLK had produced a small scale cardboard model as well as the drawings of the proposal, so it was possible for everyone to have a good idea of what the final outcome would be. Generally the scheme was well liked with most of the concerns being capable of incorporation into the design. The use of stained glass in some of the windows was accepted in principle. Following the accommodation of the various issues the Planning Submission was lodged with Havant Borough Council before Christmas with an expected final decision by the end of March 2003.

The second Christmas period in the temporary church was celebrated by the parishioners, but without the benefit of the fund raising Christmas Fair usually held in the hall. The parish had been unable to hold a number of fund raising events due to lack of facilities but had compensated in part by new ventures such as a sponsored walk, organised by John Burridge, which brought in over £1,000. Of more concern was the lack of facilities for bringing the parish together outside of the Masses, and with no apparent progress to the building site next to the hall Father Joe had to make strenuous efforts to maintain interest in the parish.

The question of cost continued to occupy the attention of the parish committee and much thought went into how costs could be reduced. Unfortunately there seemed to be as many issues increasing cost, for example the stained glass windows, as were proposed for reducing it. The detail of the design and the minutiae of the specification were now to place an onerous burden on the committee, but without this commitment no successful conclusion could be expected. Serious work was also called for in progressing the contents claim in the absence of a written inventory. Resort was made to photographs, video records and memory, mainly by John Burridge, to establish a comprehensive list of both church and presbytery items. Then came the task of proving values for these items, a not inconsiderable task when it is realised that most of the church items were unique or at best non standard objects. This was resolved by much leafing through catalogues, approaching manufacturers for quotations and seeking opinions from recognised sources. However it was to be some months before full agreement was reached with the loss adjusters.

The work of the parish committee continued apace whilst awaiting the outcome of the planning application. Chris Whiting of DLK took over as the main contact with the architects, and frequent meetings were held to settle the hundreds of details that had to be considered. Further refinements were made to conform to the liturgical requirements specified by Canon Griffiths, all with the aim of improving the effectiveness of the new church. Revisions were made to the internal layout of the plan but in essence the planning application remained unchanged. This did not prevent Havant Borough Council requiring some adjustments to the layout, particularly in relation to the trees affecting the Presbytery and the trees in Dunsbury Way and the entrance to the front of the church. These were accommodated with marginal loss to the facilities and the planning grind continued. The definitive plans were submitted to the Council in the first week of April with the hope that approval would be obtained before the end of the month. At this stage DLK were still working without a formal letter of appointment from the Diocese and were awaiting a decision to begin the Detailed Design stage. These issues were cleared at the meeting with the Diocesan Planning Committee on the 14th April and consideration was also

Birth and Rebirth of a Parish

given to the proceedings through to the tendering stage. This required work on the Bill of Quantities and raised the question of what to do if the design was still over budget. It was agreed that the tendering process should go ahead to determine whether any of the tenders would come within the budget.

Planning approval was received by the architects on the 15th May clearing the way to proceed to the tendering stage. The planned tender issue date was fixed for the 20th July and a list of eight prospective builders was produced. Six candidates were interviewed on the 2nd July by a combined parish and design team and four were selected for invitation to tender. It was felt that an extra bidder should be sought to increase the list to five and this was done. The tender package was produced at the beginning of August with a return date of the 12th September. During this time the parish committee continued to address the problem of the cost overrun for the budgeted spend which was now running at over £100,000, with a serious risk that there would be a need for a redesign.

The tenders were duly received on the 12th September and opened in the presence of representatives of the parish and diocesan planning committee. After evaluation by Malcolm Austin of Northcroft the tenders were reviewed at a meeting on the 30th September of all the interested parties including the loss adjuster. It was agreed that the tender from Brymor was the most acceptable and within the agreed budget. It was with some consternation that the members heard from Mr. Steve Aldersley, the loss adjuster, that he was not in a position to press the green button to go ahead until he had reported to the insurers. He also confounded the meeting by expressing the view that the tender from Brymor indicated that a cost deflator should be applied to the budget for the insurer's liability, which would negate any benefit received from the competitive tender. This was a situation completely unacceptable to the committee, as no matter what design savings were made, there would always be a shortfall from the insurance payout. As can be imagined, the parish committee were at a low ebb as a result of all these disclosures. It was agreed, however, to await the outcome of Mr. Aldersley's report to the insurers.

The parish committee, however, did not let the matter rest there.

Convinced that its efforts in making a design that would result in a smaller church with significant savings for the insurers should be recognised, the parish committee prepared a submission to the insurers setting out this case. This was accepted by the Diocesan planning committee, the architects and the quantity surveyor and their signatures were appended. On the 16th October the Diocesan representatives, Iain McGrory and Sean Hayes with Father Joe and Paul Hazell in attendance, met with Steve Aldersley. The outcome of this meeting was that the Loss Adjuster agreed to accept the tender of Brymor of a fraction over £1.3 million as being the basis to proceed, and he would recommend this to the insurers. However, the tender exceeded the amount of the insurer's liability by some £12,000 and this cost would fall upon the parish. It was also agreed that within this figure the contingency of approximately £43,000 would remain the responsibility of the insurers, who would have to give their sanction to any changes in the design brought about by problems in the build. The responsibility for the provisional sums allowance of £72,000 would rest with the parish who would be required to remain within this sum or foot the bill for any excesses. This effectively reduced the insurer's liability to £1.263 million plus any contingencies.

Brymor were advised that they were the preferred contractor, but that they would have to wait for the formal contract, after receiving the insurers approval, before commencing work. The insurers, through the medium of CCIA Services Ltd. finally confirmed their approval on the 19th November leaving the way clear for the letter of intent to be raised for the builder to proceed. However, apart from a presence on site, it would be January 2004 before any serious work could commence.

In the midst of all this uncertainty the parish committee continued to work to refine the specification such as determining the colour of the bricks and the fixtures and fittings. Visits took place to find suitable contractors for the stonework for the altar and font and to determine the contents for the various rooms that made up the church buildings. Organ possibilities were considered. Work continued on the contents insurance claim to establish costs for the lost items, but it was all in better heart knowing that at last a certainty of progress had been achieved.

The parish committee's role now changed somewhat from being the recipient of other peoples' ideas to determining how they would want the church and presbytery to be fitted out. Also how control would be exercised over the costs, particularly of the items included in the provisional sums, such as the altar and font, the stained glass windows, the public address system, the kitchen fittings, site security and other matters. The committee, through various individual responsibilities with associated advisors from the parish users, set out to produce lists of every item that would need to be purchased to make the church and presbytery complete. All this without knowing, at this stage, what funds would be available.

The third Christmas since the fire was celebrated by the parish in the hall. There were still no obvious signs to the parishioners that they were ever going to get a new church, although the builders were now on site, and a programme had been issued that indicated completion of the Presbytery in July and the Church in November 2004.

Building work started on the site on the 19th January and the first site meeting with the builders was held on the 22nd January. These were to be held on a regular monthly basis until completion.

By February two sub-committees had been formed. One was the Liturgical which looked after the Altar and Font areas, the organ, the worship areas, the sacristies, the children's and infants rooms and the repository. The other, the Community and Presbytery, looked after the committee room, the office, the kitchen, the lobby narthex and link, external areas and the Presbytery. Together these produced the list of required items by dint of much researching of catalogues, obtaining quotations and visits to enable a budget to be prepared. With the provisional sums in the contract covering items such as the public address system, stained glass windows, the altar and font this came to a daunting figure of over £200,000. No agreement had yet been reached with the loss adjuster for the settlement of the contents claim.

The parish committee now turned its attention to the colour scheme for the church and decided to present the proposals to the parish for general discussion. It also considered the design and specifications for the stained glass windows. It was agreed that three windows would be suitable, the Sanctuary window, the eastern wall window above the narthex and the Lady Chapel window. Because the likely cost would be greater than the amount allowed for in the provisional sums, it was decided that the windows would be an ideal basis for making an appeal for donations towards the church and a fund raising committee was formed.

With the commencement of the building process it was remarkable how smoothly progress was made. The builders were aware that the parish was not being fully recompensed by the insurers for the cost of the project and made every effort to meet the parish's desire for savings in the building process. The outcome of this was to fluctuate over the coming months, with savings identified by both the parish committee and the builder being offset as snags came up which required additional costs to rectify, but by and large the project costs were held under control to a satisfactory extent.

Initially the parish committee considered the use of coloured film inserted between the two panes of glass of the double glazed units as the basis for providing the stained glass windows to the church. This system had been used in a number of similar situations and a visit was arranged to see the installation at the Sacred Heart Church at Bordon and the nearby Cheshire Home. In the event, it was considered that the use of film did not give an adequate representation of detail in the faces of the subjects, and the committee switched its attention to the use of the traditional stained glass process where the detail could be etched or painted in. This also gave a much wider capability for the use of textures to enhance the design, but at a significant increase in cost. The designs went through a number of metamorphoses until an acceptable design specification was achieved and a supplier identified.

During April the committee received news that the Presbytery contents claim had been settled to the satisfaction of the committee, and that banking arrangements were to be put in hand to meet the requirements of the parish for procuring, in the first instance, the contents for the presbytery. This also cleared the way for ordering the electronic organ from Abinger Organs.

During May and June the audio, heating and security specifications were finalised. The church building programme was on schedule. The Presbytery build had been put back to a revised completion date of the 23rd August but was on programme.

At a crucial meeting in July, the parish committee finally reached agreement with the loss adjuster on the settlement of the contents claim for the church. The parish had to concede some points to the loss adjuster and the settlement was less than the parish had been planning for. However, by reducing the contingency allowance in the budget, it was felt there would be sufficient funds not to compromise standards in fitting out the church. Payments from the settlement were to be phased over a period of five months in line with the expected commitments by the parish. There was a sense of relief that a significant unknown had now been resolved.

The new supplier of the stained glass windows, Sunrise Stained Glass Ltd represented by John Tarrant, had produced designs to the specification prepared by the committee that were regarded as an excellent basis for development. The designs had been crystallised into the 'Angel' window for the east wall of the nave, consisting of representations of the four Archangels, St. Michael, St. Gabriel, St. Raphael and St. Uriel; the 'Sanctuary' window consisting of seven symbols representing the sacraments and two symbols of Christianity; and the Lady Chapel window depicting the Annunciation. A problem had been identified, however, in the construction of the 'Angel' window, as this was a large area of window space supporting a circular stained glass section within the general framework. This presented problems of weight which could not be resolved without significant extra cost. In the event it was decided to concentrate efforts in producing the other two windows in time for the church completion and to hold the 'Angel' window in abeyance until a later date, when the outcome from the committee's fund raising activity was more certain. The committee paid visits to the workshop of Sunrise to meet the designer, Mrs Jude Tarrant, and to refine the details of the design. It was expected that the windows would be almost the last item to be fitted into the church and there was considerable expectation as to the impact of this on the church's magnificence.

By late July and with the completion date of the 15th November drawing nearer, the committee now had to address the procurement of the long delivery items, such as the benches, to furnish the church. Father Joe was a strong proponent of purchasing from sources in Poland of which he had considerable knowledge. The committee, however, recognising that although there were potential savings, there were also significant potential risks in delivery of large and bulky items, made the decision to play safe and order from a UK supplier. Hayes and Finch Ltd, a noted church furniture maker, was selected and a comprehensive order for the supply of wooden furniture and associated articles was placed. At the same time room was left for Father Joe to procure other church items from Poland.

In late August the Presbytery was completed and handed over to the parish. Father Joe now had somewhere permanent to live. The preparatory work done in identifying the contents required to furnish the presbytery enabled a speedy completion of the fitting out and Father Joe took up residence in September. However, due to an oversight, there would be no gas supply until two weeks later. Fortunately it was still summer! The correcting of minor faults by the builders, and the process of organising the fitting out of the Presbytery, brought home to the committee the magnitude of the task of the similar but much larger operation that lay ahead on the completion of the church.

Father Joe and John Burridge made a visit to Poland and returned with a varied array of church supplies purchased at surprisingly low prices.

The Feast Day of St. Michael was celebrated on the 3rd October and Father Joe had a surprise in store for the parishioners. Up to this point the building site for the church had been 'restricted access' under the Health and Safety regulations and few people had had the chance to see what was going on inside. By this stage the church building was complete and the fitting out was being started. Father Joe had managed to obtain permission from the builders for a strictly supervised tour of the main worship areas, and this was well received by the parishioners who had stayed after Mass for refreshments celebrating the Feast Day.

The Parish Pastoral Council with Andrea Dobson in the Chair started the preparation for the celebrations on the completion of the church, which were to consist of a blessing of the foundation stone by the Bishop of Portsmouth, Rt. Rev. Crispian Hollis, on the 18th December, and an official opening by the Bishop on the 2nd February 2005. This was envisaged as being a major event with large numbers of dignitaries and invited guests to be accommodated, a significant logistical problem. Again the resources of the parish were brought to bear to tackle this task.

At the tenth builders progress meeting on the 7th October it was clear that the original completion date of the 15th November was not going to be met and an agreed new date of the 29th November was set. It was going to be a race against time for the church to be ready for the first ceremony!

By the eleventh builders progress meeting, hopefully the penultimate one, even the revised date for completion was looking doubtful and plans were devised to ensure that the church was in a working position for the ceremony on the 18th December, even if there were still unfinished items in the building programme.

The parish was going to get its new home after three and a half years. Although this had posed a major challenge to the resources of a small parish it had responded wonderfully and produced a truly magnificent new church, a major achievement for the Portsmouth Diocese, and a lasting monument to the efforts of a dedicated team. The parish now faced an even greater challenge, to restore the parish to its former glory. Although numbers had declined with the loss of the previous church, the disaster had undoubtedly brought the parishioners closer together and the heart of the parish was now much stronger. The task now was to spread that strength outwards to encompass a wider population.

The Parish Sisters

Sisters Maria and Anne-Marie

Sister Michelle

Sister Suzanne

Sister Susan

Birth and Rebirth of a Parish

Sister Christine   Sister Geraldine

Sister Marie-Therese   Sister Betty

Chapter Eight

The Parish Sisters and 'The Sisters of Merriemede'

Nuns have always played a vital part in parish life, complementing the work of the priests. This has had the greatest effect in parishes such as St. Michael's where everything was new, the population was poor and had been severed from its roots.

The important roles of Mother St. Columba and Sister Helen from the Convent of Helpers of the Holy Souls in Portsmouth has already been noted. They provided religious instruction and preparation for the Sacraments for the children. Later, after the foundation of the parish, Sister Helen set up a social bureau in the Church Hall. With the opening of the Church Father Pat saw the need for sisters who would live on the estate and make a whole time contribution to the parish. In 1969 he discussed with Bishop Worlock, who had succeeded Archbishop King as Bishop of Portsmouth, the possibility of inviting sisters to live and work in the parish. They held discussions with the Mother General of the Sisters of the Immaculate Conception, who agreed to send three sisters to work as part of the parish team at St. Michael's. The Order was founded in 1849 in Brittany to serve the Church in poor rural areas, especially through education and nursing. Over the years their aim has been to adapt to the needs of the socially deprived and to assist the local clergy or even secular authorities. At the time of the French Revolution religious orders were unpopular and unwanted by the government. In order to survive, a few sisters settled in various places in the South of England, initially in Swansea, Illfracombe and Dorchester, more recently in Southampton and Crawley. The only communities still in existence in England are at Crawley and Leigh Park, where the Sisters strive to be a presence among God's people and to be available for pastoral duties.

After lengthy discussions, Merriemede, the former home of a doctor who had moved to live away from the estate but had retained his surgery in the house, was bought by the Order. Some felt that the nuns, like the parishioners, should rent a council house but there was a long waiting list at that time. After much discussion the type of house was eventually considered less important than the use the Sisters were prepared to make of it. The Community has never regretted the choice of Merriemede as their home which they would share with the Church as a Parish House; they still live and work there today. Initially the doctors continued to use the surgery and paid rent to the Sisters. In 1985 the doctors moved into the new Havant Health Centre and the Sisters were delighted to have the use of the whole house.

In August 1970, the year in which the new church was opened in May, three sisters moved into Merriemede. They came to work closely with the priests (at that time there were three priests in the Parish). They were involved in catechetics, preparation for the Sacraments, home visiting and running clubs for groups such as young mothers and the elderly. Sisters Michelle, Anne-Marie and Suzanne were the first to arrive. They were joined at different times by Sisters Maria, Yvonne, Susan, Marie-Therese, Christine and Geraldine, the last three of whom still live and work at Merriemede. Sister Michelle taught full time at the new St. Thomas More's school until her retirement in 1989; Sister Marie-Therese was a chaplain to the Portsmouth Hospitals from 1986 until her retirement in 2000 and Sister Geraldine is still working in education, with responsibility for the special needs of fifty severely physically disabled youngsters in a comprehensive school. The others have retired from work outside the parish and are involved in various and varied activities in the parish and in the area. In 1997, Sister Anne-Marie, who had served the community for twenty seven years, retired to France. Sister Maria also returned to France after twenty years work in the parish. Both were sadly missed and a special service of thanksgiving was held for them.

Chapter Nine

Music in the Parish

From the beginning Father Pat believed that music was an essential part of the Liturgy. The early days of the parish coincided with the Second Vatican Council which decreed that Mass should now be said in the vernacular. Therefore the well loved Gregorian chants of the Ordinary of the Mass (the Kyrie, Gloria, Creed and Agnus Dei) in Latin must be replaced by English versions. This presented an enormous challenge to the clergy and congregations and many new and banal versions were hastily written and incorporated into the Liturgy. Father Pat was determined that the music used in St. Michael's would be musically appropriate and of a high standard. To this end he insisted that the new organ should be of high quality. It was his great fortune that one of the earliest parishioners was Lawrence Stephens (always known as Laurie), Deputy Head of the new St. Thomas More's school which had been opened in 1957. This had replaced the old parish school behind St. Joseph's in Havant and now served the children of Havant and Leigh Park. He had studied for some years at a seminary where his innate musical qualities were fostered. He was an outstanding organist and choirmaster and the parish benefited from his guidance for many years. He also composed a setting of the Mass in English which, while being musically appropriate, had 'catchy' tunes and rhythms and was soon learnt by the congregation.

Laurie later became Head of the School after the retirement of Mrs. May, and he and his family lived in Leigh Park where they remained until his retirement and move to the Isle of Wight in 1988. They returned to Havant in old age and the respect and affection in which he was held were palpable at his funeral Requiem in St. Joseph's in February 2003.

The Mustard Seed (Appendix 4) was written by Laurie for the first issue of the Parish magazine Wings as Father Pat was leaving and being replaced by Father Tony Llewhellin. It is an eloquent snapshot of the early days of the parish and has been kept by many of the parishioners of that time, when the Church provided the centre of life and the services the only aesthetic experience in the rather drab world in which they lived. Laurie was a tower of strength to successive priests. This was particularly appreciated by Father Llewhellin who was a considerable musician himself. After a performance in the Church of Bach's 'Jesu Joy of Man's Desiring' by Laurie and a young oboist member of the parish, he wrote to the parents of the oboist as follows, *"Listening to her last night I remembered being introduced to 'Jesu Joy' when I was nine. The organist, when sober, had a remarkable sense of registration and played the Obligato very quietly , using the oboe stop, just the right tonal contrast with the left hand and the pedal lines. We haven't got an oboe stop in the Deanery, but we have a REAL oboe, played with a sensitivity that captures the spirituality of Bach's writing. If only we could sing with the same perception; however, in spite of our ragged edges, we enjoy trying".*

In 1989 Jim Berry, a cellist and musician who had retired to Rowlands Castle, was persuaded by Father Turbitt to help with choir practices by playing the piano for them. Very soon he was urged to attempt the organ and to direct the choir. He attended a four day course for 'reluctant organists'; i.e. pianists who had been thrown in at the deep end. The tutor told him that 2,000 people had passed through her hands, an indication of the new way of celebration of the Liturgy ordained by the Second Vatican Council. Lay participation through hymns and new settings of the Mass were the order of the day. This change was difficult for some older people who missed the beauty of the Gregorian Chant sung in Latin and the Latin hymns sung at Benediction. Some priests were sensitive to their feelings and continued to have one quiet Mass when no hymns were sung. It was to be many years before congregational singing during Mass became the norm and the lack of musical expertise in many congregations only emphasised the problem. The love of the old Latin hymns was not confined to the educated classes but also encompassed many people who had been singing them since childhood. It is still a problem today and the Church authorities are still struggling to find ways in which singing during Mass adds to, rather than distracts from, its meaning. An essential in every parish is a competent musician to lead the congregation and to train the choir to perform chants of real musical quality at important occasions and feasts. This applies most particularly to the ceremonies of Holy Week. Jim Berry's first Mass playing the organ was Maundy Thursday 1989, followed by Good Friday, Holy Saturday and Easter Sunday. He writes *"there was no escape after that!"*

At that time the Folk Choir (organised by Bob Sillence and Ron Snelling) used to sing at 11 o'clock Mass on the first Sunday of every month and sometimes on other occasions. This provided an outlet for younger people who liked to sing music akin to that which they enjoyed in their lives outside the Church.

The main choir sang at the 11 o'clock Masses on the remaining Sundays. At that time the sung items on a normal Sunday consisted of the entrance hymn, Lord have mercy, Glory to God, the Psalm, the Alleluia (including the verse), the Offertory hymn, a motet (sometimes replaced by an organ piece), Holy Holy Holy, the acclamation 'Through Him, with Him, in Him', the Our Father, Lamb of God, the Communion hymn, occasionally another motet and the Recessional hymn. Most of this fell to the choir; the Psalm, the Alleluia verse and motet had to be different each week and sorted out at weekly choir practice. No wonder Jim Berry found it daunting! The standard set by Laurie Stephens was far above that of most parishes at that time, let alone one where some members of the choir had little or no musical experience and were unable to read music. Jim Berry remembers that choir practices were enhanced by teas provided by Martha O'Connell; they sometimes seemed to be more important than the singing!

For various reasons both the senior choir and the folk choir disbanded in 1994 and the next landmark in parish music was the arrival of Rosemary Field. She and her husband, Mark Dancer, both Catholics and professionally qualified organists, came to live in the area when Rosemary was appointed to the post of Church Music Advisor to the Anglican Church in East Hampshire, West Sussex and the Isle of Wight. There was an ecumenical dimension to the post which permitted her to assist with the music of churches of other denominations. She sought a Mass time early enough to enable her to go to other churches as part of her job. She writes *"St. Michael's fitted the bill and it was not long before Father Felix had found out I was a musician. Together we made plans to establish a singing group at the Church. It soon became impossible to restrict the work at St. Michael's to the amount of time that the Church would have been eligible for within the terms of my job, so it progressed to being a bigger, but voluntary, commitment. Volunteers were asked for, and several came forward – five sopranos, two altos, three tenors (of whom two were glamour ladies!) and a couple of basses, including Jim Berry, the organist. Some read music, others not, and the degree of effort and quantity of time they put into learning things from tapes and in freezing rehearsals was very great and a credit to their devotion. We were ambitious within our limitations and very soon gathered some extra members who brought with them family connections. Thus at Christmas we could gather the little band of flute, guitar, cello, viola and keyboard. We soon found that the pews, lacking anywhere to put all the music copies, were inadequate and , when my husband's church was disposing of some choir stalls we bought them. This brought its own problems – no kneelers! So we bought some heavy-duty foam and miles of deep rose velvet and constructed a sort of cover for the foam. Much fun was had in trying to stack all this kit in the minute cupboard under the organ. It became less hazardous once we installed a battery-light! Throughout this time we sang only for major festivals and for the odd 'extra'. A highlight for me was an Advent carol service one year; one or two moving Good Fridays also stick in the mind. We knew how to celebrate; flowers and chocolates were often exchanged and many a time after a term of nagging and cajoling them they presented me with fantastic flowers arranged by Halina.* (For many years the Church flowers have been done by Halina Absalom). *What stays with me is their kindness, tolerance and perseverance. A real team spirit operated and each person did what they could – me as a teacher and the team learning some quite demanding things which were right outside their previous experience."*

For members of the congregation this was indeed a heyday which, sadly, had to end in 1999 when Rosemary's contract ended and she had to move. Despite efforts she made to ensure continuity, alternative arrangements did not work out. At one parish meeting Rosemary said she didn't want to call the singing group a choir because when she inevitably had to move on it would leave a choir-shaped hole! Perhaps somewhere within the new church another musician will appear.

The enforced move into the temporary Church after the fire has meant that Jim Berry has had to make do with a home-style electronic organ. None of the others who had previously played the organ for hymns sung at Mass (principally Chris Moule who had been Jim's deputy for several years) had any familiarity with this type of instrument.

The organ that was destroyed in the fire was a magnificent pipe organ, worth more than £100,000 at the time of its destruction. Sadly the insurance cover for this instrument was limited to £53,498 and this negated the installation of a similar replacement. However, developments in recent years in electronic organs have meant that the replacement organ is a magnificent instrument in its own right and it is well placed to continue the fine tradition of music at St. Michael's.

The Crucifix above the High Altar

The Celtic Cross in the High Altar

*The Tabernacle,
the IHS and the
PX symbols*

*The Ambo
and the Alpha and
Omega Symbol*

Chapter Ten

Symbols and Sacred Images in the Church

In our present age of newspapers, television, computers and road signs, we are bombarded by so many symbols every day that we take for granted the message they bring.

However, when we enter a church, especially an old one, we see many symbols and emblems carved upon the stonework and the woodwork, and many images in the stained glass, pictures and tapestries; yet rarely do we understand the significance of these symbols and their deeper meaning.

This chapter is an introduction to ancient Christian symbology and art to help the visitor to our new Church of St. Michael and All Angels to understand the significance of the various symbols and images, their history and meaning.

Every Christian church is profoundly symbolic through its own shape as a building, usually in the form of a cross of one shape or another. Within the building there will be triangular structures supporting the roof and circular structures in the window frames. Each of the fundamental shapes of the circle, triangle, square, hexagon and cross has a deep religious and physical significance stemming from ancient times. This chapter shows an illustration of each of these symbols found within our Church and gives a short explanation of their deeper meaning.

The Christian art in every church has one major purpose, to bring those who enter God's house into spiritual communion with the Lord, through inducing a sense that He is present.

In our new Church, we have tried to create a spiritual atmosphere and a sense of welcoming light, airiness and warmth through our use of colour. Reds, purple and golden yellows predominate. The colours themselves are highly symbolic.

Because it is impossible and indeed irreverent to represent the invisible and incomprehensible God by a single image, and forbidden to worship Him as an idol, all references to God in the ancient Christian Church were through symbols and allusion. For instance the ancient

Greeks alluded to God through the symbols of Alpha and Omega, the beginning and end of all things, which are carved on the Ambo from which God's word is delivered.

The other symbols in Christian art represent Christ as the Son of God, the Blessed Mary ever-Virgin as the Mother of God, the Saints, the Angels, the Trinity, the Holy Spirit and the Sacraments.

The Church layout

The interior of the Church is essentially cruciform in shape with the Choir on the left and the Blessed Sacrament Chapel on the right forming the transepts. The Sanctuary at the head of the Nave is the sacred portion of the Church in which the Altar stands. The High Altar is a permanent fixture in the centre of the Sanctuary. The Credence is a shelf or table in the Sanctuary upon which hosts and other liturgical items rest until used at the altar. The Lectern or Ambo is a stand in the Sanctuary on which rests the Lectionary or Bible from which the Word of God is read. The Paschal Candle, usually situated in the Sanctuary, is a candle lit on Easter Eve and extinguished on Ascension Day. When the Candle is situated in the Baptistry in the celebration of the sacrament of Baptism it serves to remind us of our own baptism.

The High Altar contains the Relic of Saint Anthony of Padua. (Appendix 8) Usually the Relic is held in a reliquary placed on the Altar. In St. Michael's the Relic is set in the centre of the Celtic Cross within the Altar.

The Blessed Sacrament Chapel to the right of the Sanctuary, and the Lady Chapel on the left of the nave, are used for private prayer and the weekday services. The Blessed Sacrament Chapel is seen to be connected with the Sanctuary by using the same colour of carpet leading to the Tabernacle. This is a locked safe for the reservation of the Sacrament where the Body of Christ is present at all times, indicated by a red light in the Lamp as a reminder of that presence.

The Choir, to the left of the Sanctuary, is the part of the Church used by the Choristers and the Organist.

The Lantern is the open tower above the altar from which the Crucifix

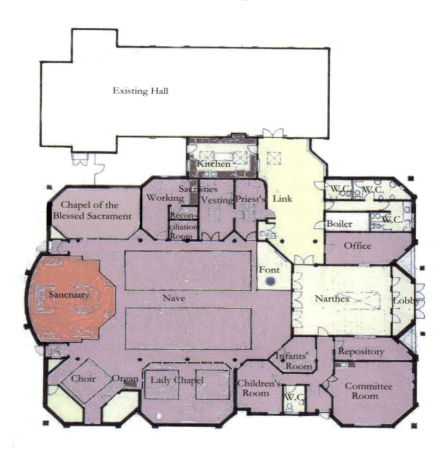

Ground Plan of the Church of St. Michael and All Angels

is suspended. The light from the Lantern shines down upon the Altar as God looks upon the sacrifice of the Mass and the prayer ascends as incense to Heaven.

The Nave is the central division of the Church in which the congregation is seated.

The Baptistry at the entrance to the nave contains the Font, which holds the water for Baptism and for those who enter to make the sign of the Cross as a reminder of belonging to the Church through baptism.

The Narthex is the vestibule or closed-in porch across the building at the rear of the nave from which entrance is gained to the Church and is also the area for welcoming and gathering.

The Sacristies are the places where the clergy vest and where the sacred vessels and vestments are kept secure. There are separate sacristies for the priest, preparing the liturgy and for the altar servers.

The Symbols within the Church

The Latin Cross is the most commonly used form of cross and is principally represented in the Church by the Crucifix above the High Altar.

The Greek Cross is a cross with all the arms of equal length and is found in the doors and furniture of the Church.

The Jerusalem or Crusader's Cross usually has four small crosses between the arms of the larger cross, the five crosses together symbolising the five wounds of Our Lord. This was worn by Geoffrey de Bouillon, the first ruler of Jerusalem after the liberation from the Moslems. This form is included in the Celtic Cross in the Altar.

The Celtic Cross, or the Cross of Iona, dates back to the early centuries of the Christian era. It was said to have been taken from what is now Ireland to the island of Iona by Columba in the 6th Century. This form of cross is carved on the front of the High Altar.

The Chi Rho, a monogram of the Greek word for Christ using the first two letters Chi (X) and Rho (R). This symbol is carved into the stonework of the support for the Tabernacle in the Blessed Sacrament Chapel.

Alpha and Omega are the first and last letters of the Greek alphabet. They are used to represent God as the beginning and the end of all things. This symbol is carved on the front of the Ambo.

I.N.R.I. are the initial letters for the Latin inscription on the Crucifix "Iesus Nazarenus Rex Iudaeorum": Jesus of Nazareth, King of the Jews.

The Equilateral Triangle is a symbol of the Trinity. The three distinct angles combine to make one complete figure. The Circle stands for eternity as it is without beginning and without end. The two figures combined suggest the eternity of the Trinity. This symbol is found in the triangular window above the Narthex.

The Three Intertwining Circles indicate the doctrine of the equality, unity and coeternal nature of the three persons of the Trinity. This symbol is found in the woodwork and furniture of the Church.

The Lamp in the Blessed Sacrament Chapel is another symbol of the Word of God and the presence of Jesus in the Blessed Sacrament.

The Candlestick suggests our Lord's words "I am the light of the world". When two candlesticks are used they also represent His two-fold nature, human and divine.

There are a number of symbols woven into the fabric of the vestments and cloths used for the ceremonies. These include:

The Lily, a symbol of Easter and immortality. The bulb decays in the ground yet from it new life is released.

The Palm Leaf. In ancient times a palm leaf was given to winners in contests of strength and skill. With Christians it signifies the heavenly reward. (Revelations 7:9)

The Bursting Pomegranate, a symbol of the Resurrection and the power of our Lord who was able to come forth from the tomb.

The Christmas Rose, a symbol of the Nativity and of Messianic prophesies.

The Grapes signify the sacrament of the Eucharist and are most commonly found about the Communion table.

The Stained Glass Windows

The Sanctuary Window, of circular shape, is divided into nine segments. Two represent symbols of Christianity and seven represent the seven Sacraments. Clockwise from the top the first symbol is the Font representing the sacrament of Baptism. The second segment comprises a stole draped over a prie dieu representing the sacrament of Penance and Reconciliation. The third segment is the Lamb, a symbol of the Resurrection and the holding of the seven seals of the future of the Church (Revelations 5:1). The fourth segment shows the Dove rising from seven flames. The Dove is the symbol for the Holy Spirit and the seven flames the gifts of the Holy Spirit, together representing the sacrament of Confirmation. The fifth segment is the intertwined rings representing the sacrament of Marriage. The sixth segment is an illustration of the book and key representing the sacrament of Holy Orders. On one side of the open book are the intertwined letters PX or "Persona Christi"; on the other side the symbol of the Greek Cross representing the carrying of the Cross into the Priesthood. The seventh segment shows the fish, a secret sign used by the persecuted early Christians to designate themselves as believers in Jesus. The initial letters for the Greek words for "Jesus Christ, God's Son, Saviour" spell the Greek word for fish. The symbol "**IHS**" is the first three letters (iota, eta and sigma) of the Greek word spelling Jesus. The eighth segment, a flask of oil with the letters "OI" inscribed standing for "Olio Infirmorum" represents the sacrament of the Anointing of the Sick. The centre and ninth segment, the chalice with the host above, represents the sacrament of the Eucharist, the centre of the life of a Christian. Overall, the window assumes the outline of a rose within which is a blue, Greek style cross reminiscent of the Blue Tiled Cross of the old Church which was destroyed in the fire.

The Lady Chapel window represents the Annunciation, the appearance of the Archangel Gabriel to Our Lady to proclaim that she will be the Mother of Our Lord and Saviour.

It is intended there will be further stained glass windows in both the Blessed Sacrament Chapel and above the Narthex.

The window above the Narthex will represent St. Michael and the other archangels Gabriel, Raphael and Uriel. Of special significance is St. Michael as he has been invoked as patron and protector of the Church from the time of the Apostles. The Eastern Rite, and many others, place him over all angels as the Prince of the Seraphim. He is described as the "chief of princes" and as the leader of the forces of Heaven in the triumph over Satan. The angel Gabriel first appeared in the Old Testament in the prophecies of Daniel when he announced the prophecy of seventy weeks (Daniel 9:21-27). He appeared to Zechariah to announce the birth of St. John the Baptist (Luke 1:11) and he proclaimed the Annunciation of Mary to be the Mother of our Lord and Saviour (Luke 1:26). The angel Raphael first appeared in the Book of Tobit (Tobias 3:25, 5:5-28, 6:12) and announced "I am the Angel Raphael, one of the seven who stand before the throne of God." (Tobias 12:15) St. Raphael is the guardian angel of all humanity. St. Uriel whose name means "God is my light" is considered to be the interpreter of prophesy.

The four windows in the Blessed Sacrament Chapel will represent the Evangelists, Sts. Matthew, Mark, Luke and John. St. Matthew is shown as a Winged Creature with a man's face. The winged man represents St. Matthew because his Gospel traces Jesus' human genealogy. The Winged Creature with a lion's face is the symbol for St. Mark because his Gospel begins with "The voice of one crying in the wilderness" and this suggests the roar of a lion. St. Luke, "The Winged Creature with the head of an ox", is symbolised by the ox, the animal of sacrifice, since St. Luke stresses the atoning sacrifice of Jesus. The high soaring eagle is the emblem of St. John, "The Winged Creature with an eagle's head", because in his narrative he rises to the loftiest heights interpreting the mind of Christ.

Vestments

The Church's liturgical year starts from Advent as the preparation for Christmas (and for the Second Coming of Christ) followed by Ordinary Time, then Lent, Easter and Ordinary Time again. Each period, together with other feasts occurring throughout the year, is associated with its own colour, both for the Church decoration and the ministers' vestments.

Purple The liturgical colour for both Advent and Lent symbolises penitence and mourning. It is also symbolic of death and is used for funerals.

Blue As in the colour of the sky, blue is symbolic of Heaven. It is also the colour identified with Our Lady. It can be used as a symbol of truth.

Green Represents the triumph of life over death. Green is also the symbol of growth in Christian life. It is used mostly in Ordinary Time. In some traditions it is the liturgical colour of the season of the Trinity.

White The colour of purity, it is used in baptism as it represents grace and cleansing from sin.

Red Because it is the colour of blood it is used to symbolise the commemoration of the martyred saints. It is also used as the colour for Pentecost as it is the colour of fire and is therefore connected to the "flame-like" love of the Holy Spirit.

Yellow Is a universal symbol for the spiritual presence of God as true and good. As the colour of light it may also symbolise divinity.

Brown A symbol of spiritual death and degradation, it is seldom used in the liturgy.

Grey The colour of ash, grey may be used during Lent to represent repentance and sorrow. Sometimes grey is used to express the mortality of the body and the immortality of the spirit, since grey is a shade between black and white.

Priests serving Leigh Park

Father Murphy O'Connor   *Father John Keenan*

Father Pat Lyons

Birth and Rebirth of a Parish

Father Hishon with Jo and Les Cannell

Father Dominic Golding

Priests serving Leigh Park

Father Peter Turbitt

Father Tom McGrath　　　　*Father John Dunne*

Priests serving Leigh Park

Father Joseph Keller   Father Jozef Gruszkiewicz

Father John O'Shea with Laurie Stephens

Appendix 1

Priests serving Leigh Park from St. Joseph's Havant 1950 to 1966

SCANTLEBURY Robert E.	1950 – 1962
MURPHY William	1962 – 1966

Priests serving Leigh Park 1966 to 2004

Parish Priests

MURPHY-O'CONNOR Patrick J.	1966 – 1971
LLEWHELLIN Anthony	1971 – 1976
LYONS Patrick	1976 – 1981
HISHON Ronald	1981 – 1983
TURBITT Peter	1983 – 1989
MUSCAT Felix	1989 – 1997
GOLDING Dominic	1998
KELLER Joseph	1998 – 2001
GRUSZKIEWICZ Jozef	2001 –

Assistant Priests

KEENAN John	1966 – 1969
DUNNE John	1969 – 1973
O'SHEA John	1971 – 1973
McGRATH Thomas	1973 – 1977
McELHINNEY Joseph	1977 – 1978
McAULIFFE James M.	1982 – 1983

Deacons

CHADWICK John (Ordained 1995)	1991 – 1995

Birth and Rebirth of a Parish

Appendix 2

Papal and Diocesan Awards

Richard Gill	Papal Award	
Lawrence Stephens	Diocesan Medal	
Sister Michelle	Diocesan Medal	
Coralie Carter	Diocesan Medal	
Robert Carter	Diocesan Medal	
Martha O'Connell	Diocesan Medal	
Reuben 'Alex' Alexander	Diocesan Medal	
John Burridge	Pro Ecclesia et Pontifice	1999
	Guild of St. Stephen Siver Medal	1968
	Guild of St. Stephen Gold Medal	2001

Martha O'Connell and John Burridge display their awards

Appendix 3

Works of Art in the Old Church

Crucifix

Made by J.L. Jezierski and installed when the church was built in 1970. See Chapter Three. This objet d'art was lost when the Church was destroyed in 2001.

Stations of the Cross

The Stations of the Cross were damaged in the fire that destroyed the Church in 2001. The cost of refurbishment was considered to be too great to be borne by the insurance comany and a further set was commissioned in 2003.

Icon of St. Michael

In 1997 the mosaic panel of St. Michael, made by Dom Paul Linus and Dom Charles Norris of Buckfast Abbey, was unveiled and blessed by Father Charles Norris. The cost to the Parish was £6,000. This item was recovered from the fire and reinstalled in the new Church in 2004.

Book of Remembrance

In 1992 Father Felix ordered this from Farnborough Abbey at a cost of £250. Brother Cuthbert worked the calligraphy. The names of all deceased parishioners from 1966 were included. The total cost of the project, including the bookcase, was £1,200. The book was blessed on All Souls Day 1992 in the presence of members of the Murphy O'Connor family.

Icon of Our Lady of the Holy Land

This icon was purchased by a parish group during a visit to the Holy Land during Fr. Peter Turbitt's incumbency and is now installed in the new Church.

*The Blue Tiled Cross
by J.L. Jezierski*

The Icon of St. Michael

*The Icon of Our Lady
of the Holy Land*

The Book of Remembrance

Appendix 4

The Mustard Seed

Extract from a 1971 issue of 'Wings', the Parish magazine, written by Laurie Stephens.

The first houses to go up in Leigh Park were in that part of Purbrook Way which now stretches westward from Riders Lane past Ditcham Crescent. This was about 1948. All the rest of the estate was fields, trees, a few farmhouses and the Cricketers. Men went to work on a bus that ran once an hour, women pushed their prams to a derelict Army Camp in West Leigh to buy groceries, and the few Catholics walked to Mass at St. Joseph's in Havant, where a white-haired old priest, Canon Bailey, always gave Holy Communion before Mass. He died and Canon Scantlebury became parish priest in February 1950. By 1952 the growth of Leigh Park had made the parish too big for one priest. Canon Scantlebury went to the seminary at Wonersh, chose a student he liked the look of and then told Bishop King he wanted a curate. In July the student, now a priest, arrived. It was Father Targett and very quickly the Catholics of Leigh Park felt they had a priest of their own. Father Targett, who had been a magician in the variety halls and later a prisoner of war, worked among us with such untiring dedication that many older Catholics remember that time with great nostalgia.

He soon found us our own 'church', a Nissen hut abandoned by the Navy. It was somewhere between Swanmore Road and Winterslow Drive, at that time just trees and narrow lanes that were ankle deep in mud in winter. We sat on hard benches, smoked out if we lit the stove, frozen if we didn't, while the condensation dripped on us from the roof. We watched the priest at the dull brown triptych altar brightened by a white altar cloth embroidered in red and we enjoyed the presence of God.

About 1954 the Archbishop was persuaded by Canon Scantlebury (he seems to have had a way with him) to buy the site of the present church for the future Leigh Park parish. The Hall was built by Marchetti for a Mass centre and dedicated to Blessed Margaret Pole. We did all the things Catholics like doing for their church. The women polished the floor; the men put up a notice board; we even had a male voice choir for Holy Week. Rumours began that Father Targett was to be our parish priest but nothing came of it.

In 1957 a third priest arrived, young and smiling – Father Bennett. In 1958 Father Targett (sadly) left us and Father Dobbin took his place. Then in 1962 Canon Scantlebury, who had grown tired of counting all the pennies in the Leigh Park collections, went to Brockenhurst and Father Murphy arrived. He surprised us by entertaining us all (about 1,000) to dinner at the Savoy (sic) in Southsea as a way of getting more money in the plate on Sunday mornings. Father Dobbin was replaced by Father Richer, very tall and thin, and he in turn by Father Keenan.

During those years our longing for a 'proper' church grew. We wanted to be a parish. And in 1966 it happened. Father Murphy O'Connor came from Winchester and after a few weeks was made parish priest, with Father Keenan as curate. The rest of the story is well known – the plans and discussions for the new church, the group meetings and house Masses, the talks with Anglicans and Methodists, the broadcast of Mass from the Hall, the guitar playing and the funny songs, the laying of the foundation stone in 1969, and at last the opening, in great splendour, of the Church of Saint Michael and All Angels on May 15th, 1970, and the tremendous party at Tampax in the evening. The mustard seed had indeed grown, and when Mass was televised in colour from our Church, we felt proud, happy, and above all, grateful to our exciting parish priest.

But of course it could not last forever. At a sad-happy party organised by tireless Father Dunne last September, Father Pat and Father O'Shea said good-bye to us.

The next Sunday a new priest stared at us through thick glasses, and told us he was a Welshman from Southsea who had Hell in his name. And we thought, 'Perhaps life won't be so bad after all.'

Lawrence Stephens

Birth and Rebirth of a Parish

Appendix 5

An Appreciation of John Burridge

St. Michael's has been blessed with a number of lay people who have made significant contributions to the parish, some of whom are mentioned in this book, and others who have made their contributions unsung. However there is one person, whose presence for almost thirty-five years, has done more than anyone in recent times to hold the parish together in the difficult times that it has experienced over the years. As Master of Ceremonies John has maintained an uncompromising regime over the young servers ensuring that the liturgical requirements have been kept to a high standard. His service has been recognised twice with the award of the Silver Medal of the Guild of St. Stephen as long ago as 1968 and in more recent times the award of the Gold Medal in 2001. He was awarded the 'Pro Ecclesia et Pontifice' in 1999. He has been the undisputed right hand man to numerous priests, both permanent and visiting.

John has been a tireless worker for the Church in all manner of activities. He has chaired the Parish Pastoral Council for more years than probably any other person in the history of St. Michael's Church. He was a crucial member of the Parish Rebuilding Committee taking the lead in all the liturgical aspects including the design of the stonework for the altar and ambo. He invariably leads the team that runs the annual parish fairs and has organised other fund raising activities, notably the annual Parish sponsored walk which raises on average over £1,000 per annum. He also has the dubious talent for fixing the rainiest day in August for the walk!

His main strength, for which the Parish has the most to thank him, is holding the Parish together in the difficult times when there was no regular priest. He organised temporary stand-ins, and when this was not possible led the parishioners in Eucharistic Services in place of Mass. He was a focal point, in the absence of a priest, to whom everyone looked and was never found wanting.

Appendix 6

Parishioners who have chaired the Parish Council

(not in chronological order)

Lawrence Stephens
Jimmy Kirby
Dick Gill
Joyce King
Tom Leahy
Bob Carter
John Brogden
Carole Maddock
Archie Smith
John Burridge
Andrea Dobson

Appendix 7

Letters of Support and Donations following the loss of the Church in 2001

Havant Borough Council – Development Control Committee.

Commander A.C.W. Jones, RN, Wade Court, Havant.

St. Richard's Catholic Primary School, Chichester.

Arun Community Church, Rustington, W. Sussex.

Fr. P. D. Turbitt, Wantage, Oxon.

Rev. Dominic Golding, Church of St. James & St. William of York, Reading.

Revd. Alan W. Bennett, Area Dean of Wendover, Bucks.

Fr. Tom McGrath, St. Joseph's, Maidenhead, Berks.

St. Philip's Church, Cosham, Hants.

Mr. and Mrs. K. Grant, Chichester.

Councillor June Hanan, Battins Ward, Havant.

Parish of Sacred Heart, Lambourn and Our Lady of Lourdes, Hungerford, Berks.

Rev. E. Richer, Southampton

Botley Drive Methodist Church.

St. Michael and All Angels, Paulsgrove.

Fr. David Whitehead, The Catholic Church in Stubbington and Lee-on-the-Solent.

Fr. Kieron O'Brien, The Parish of Chichester.

Drusilla Wieloch, Putney Heath, London.

Parish of St. Wilfred, Cowplain, Waterlooville.

The Rev. Mike Sheffield, St. Albans Church, West Leigh.

St. Faith's Church, Havant.

The Rev. J.R. Humphreys, St. Edmund's Catholic Church, Horndean.

Rev. Cyril Murtagh, Petersfield, Hants.

St. John the Baptist Church, Rowlands Castle.

Appendix 8

The Relic of St. Anthony of Padua.

The High Altar of St. Michael and All Angels contains a relic of St. Anthony of Padua set in the centre of the Celtic Cross.

Anthony was born in Lisbon in 1195 and was baptised Ferdinand. He was educated at the Lisbon Cathedral School and joined the Canons Regular of St. Augustine (Augustinians) when he was fifteen and stayed in the St. Vincent Convent. He then went to the Santa Croce Convent, Coimbra, where he devoted himself to the study of the Sacred Scriptures, the works of the Fathers and prayer.

Ferdinand was inspired by five Franciscan martyrs. He resolved to become a Friar Minor so that he might also preach the Faith. He received the Franciscan habit at Santa Croce and took the name Anthony.

After Anthony attended the General Chapter at Assisi in May 1221 he went on to stay at the hermitage of Montepaolo (near Forli) where he continued his studies and his life of prayer.

St. Francis, in 1224, then asked Anthony to teach theology at Bologna, Montpellier and Toulouse. Anthony continued to gain a reputation as an orator and preached against various heresies. Through the latter he gained the title of Malleus Hereticorum (Hammer of the Heretics) and he helped many to convert.

After Francis died on the 3rd October 1226, Anthony returned to Italy and was elected Minister Provincial of Emilia. He resigned in May 1230 and moved to the Convent of Padua. During his time in Padua Anthony gained a great reputation due to his dedication to justice and his care of the poor.

Anthony retired to Camposanpiero, near Padua, where he became seriously ill and died on the 13th June 1231. He was canonised on the 30th May 1232 by Pope Gregory IX and was given the title of 'Evangelical Doctor'. Anthony's relics were transferred to a church in Padua, built by the people in 1263, the place with which he is chiefly associated.

Birth and Rebirth of a Parish

Acknowledgements

It is impossible to thank individually all those who have contributed to the life of the Parish and to the writing of this History. Some are mentioned in the text; others, equally deserving, are not. We thank them all. We are grateful for the kind support given us by the printers, The Better Book Company Ltd, The Portsmouth News for permission to reproduce part of the front page of the newspaper of the 4th July 2001 and to all other contributors of photographs who have permitted their reproduction. We are also grateful to Father Jozef for writing the chapter on the Symbols and Sacred Images in the Church, and to Bishop Crispian and the Diocese for their support throughout.